CN00543657

FUSED

A memoir of childhood OCD and adult obsession

Fused: A memoir of childhood OCD and adult obsession

Written by Dr James Manning

Published by the West Suffolk CBT Service
Angel Corner
8 Angel Hill
Bury St Edmunds
Suffolk
England

ELIGE COGNISCERE

FUSED: A memoir of childhood OCD and adult obsession

Written by

Dr James Manning, ClinPsyD

Published by The West Suffolk CBT Service Ltd

Acknowledgements

I very much appreciate the help of my partner Nicola who has read through and corrected several drafts of this book. I greatly value her informed opinion and deep knowledge of psychology. She has not only helped me personally, but added significantly to the quality of this book. I wouldn't have been able to produce this work without her. Thanks also to my children Christabelle and Harvey for coping with my increased levels of unavailability.

I am very grateful to my parents, Mary and Jim, who brought me up and who have been an incredible support to me. It is very difficult to live with others with mental health problems, and my parents were very accepting of my difficulties over the years. Many thanks for similar reasons to my friend, since childhood, James Whitman, and my siblings Marian and Paul.

Thanks to Dr Peter Appleton and Celia Graham who currently supervise my clinical work, and who helped me to draw out ideas for this book. Nick Hodgson did a great job on copyediting this book: so thanks for your hard work on polishing it Nick. The proofreading was completed by Paul Lancaster: I am fortunate to have access to your eagle eyes to correct all of those typos. Thanks also to Max V for his encouraging advice.

The author

Dr James Manning is a Consultant Clinical Psychologist and Managing Director of the West Suffolk CBT Service, Bury St Edmunds, Suffolk, England.

James has postgraduate qualifications in both Clinical Psychology and Counselling Psychology. He has written several self-help books, and is co-author of the multiple award winning book, *'A Journey with Panic'*.

Also by Dr James Manning

Think About Your Thinking to Stop Depression

How to Help Your Loved One Overcome Depression

*Think About Your Thinking – Cognitive Behaviour
Therapy Program for Depression*

CBT for Panic Attacks

The Little Book on CBT for Depression

*Cognitive Behaviour Therapy for Social Anxiety
and Shyness.*

*A Simple Introduction to Cognitive Behaviour Therapy
for Visual Learners.*

CBT Worksheets

CBT: What it is and How it Works (2nd Edition)

My CBT Journal

CBT Worksheets for Anxiety

CBT Worksheets for Teenage Social Anxiety

Breaking Free from Social Anxiety

A Journey with Panic

Fused

Contents

Preface

The word fused has many connotations. Depending on its context, fused could mean primed and ready to explode; to be enmeshed with something; or that an internal wire in a machine has burnt out. For me, all these definitions apply in some way to obsessive compulsive disorder (OCD).

I first heard the term 'fused' being talked about when I was in peer supervision. Dr Nicola Ridgeway, now a Consultant Clinical Psychologist, was describing the experiences of some of her clients with OCD. She reported that her clients were 'fused' to ideas or feelings. It was as if Nicola's clients couldn't detach themselves from thoughts or feelings that were making them feel miserable. Nicola seemed at her happiest when she was helping her clients to free themselves from being stuck.

I identified very much with what Nicola's clients were going through. As a child I regularly got stuck or enmeshed with things. It was as if I was covered in the stickiest fly-paper possible. Going through my daily life things kept sticking to me: thoughts, ideas, images and passing comments from others. I found that I just couldn't shake things off. As I grew older so many frightening thoughts, images, and ideas got stuck to me that I couldn't really see who I was anymore.

I have already written a few books in the self-help field and a little while ago I decided to write a book about OCD. Initially, I couldn't think of the best way to approach it, so I just started writing. After a while, I realised that what was coming together was an autobiography: an unadulterated autobiography of my experience of OCD. As I continued to write, I asked myself, 'Should I continue this? I'm a Consultant Clinical Psychologist, a highly trained and responsible person. A person who runs a service. Will I lose credibility by 'coming out' about my OCD and sharing my most painful and intimate problems with others? Isn't it a bit of a professional risk?'

Well, I guess you will decide that for yourself when you read this book. The most poignant feedback I have received so far has been from my partner Nicola who looked over the book and said, 'Wow...I didn't realise ... *just...* how disturbed you were!'

But, as you notice, you have this book in front of you right now, so I didn't take what Nicola said in a negative way. As a psychologist I have a very different view on emotional dysfunction to most people. Our weirdest and most frightening thoughts retain their power when we keep them hidden, and shame is a very powerful silencer! How can I possibly expect other people who I work with to be open and frank about their problems if I'm not transparent about mine?

Introduction

Experts still don't really know what causes OCD, although most agree that it runs in families. At the moment researchers think that it probably comes about through a combination of learnt behaviour, genetic vulnerability, and brain developmental problems in the womb and/or in childhood. Although OCD affects only a small proportion of the population – between 1 and 2 percent – the number of those who are actually affected by OCD is much higher. OCD sufferers will recognise that anyone they have a relationship with, whether it's their parent, their child, their sibling, their partner, their boss, or their employee, will also be affected by their OCD. OCD comes with you as part of a package wherever you go!

The main thing that separates OCD sufferers from people without it, is that OCD sufferers find it very difficult to separate themselves from frightening and intrusive thoughts, images, and feelings. There is also an accompanying compulsion to reduce the intensity of the emotional experience by carrying out specific behaviours or thinking patterns. Psychologists have a name for these compulsive responses; they call them 'neutralisers'.

Intrusive thoughts

I didn't have a word for intrusive thoughts until I started my clinical training. I simply recognised that I had certain thoughts that were a bit like anti-social hooligans compared with my other thoughts. These thoughts seemed to be disrespectful of the natural order of other thoughts. My intrusive thoughts tended to contain frightening images or ideas and would simply barge their way into my awareness whenever they felt like it. To most people, even without OCD, such thoughts will feel familiar. They don't wait around patiently until you're not busy, like your other thoughts do. They can pop into your mind while you're having a conversation with someone, working, watching TV, or travelling. They're usually accompanied with quite intense emotion, mainly anxiety or guilt.

Experts suggest that people who experience OCD are much more vulnerable to intrusive thoughts. They suggest that OCD sufferers have more of these thoughts because a part of the brain called the caudate nucleus doesn't forge connections too well with other areas of the brain. If you haven't heard of the caudate nucleus, it sits deep inside the brain and is supposed to operate a bit like a mental filter. Part of its job is to act as a doorkeeper, screening the mind for relevant information, deciding what to let in and what to keep out. In people with OCD, the caudate nucleus doesn't have a good ability to determine what's real and what isn't, and it tends to let in all kinds of strange or frightening thoughts that it shouldn't. The result is like being in a rough nightclub without a doorperson.

I was plagued with intrusive thoughts as a child. For me, experiencing regular frightening thoughts was part of my normal existence. I didn't realise that things could be any different. I didn't stop to think for one minute whether they happened to others as well.

It wasn't until I was training as a clinical psychologist that I found out why people with OCD get more stuck with their intrusive thoughts than people without it.

The cingulate gyrus is a small part of the sub-cortical region – based deep inside the brain – and is supposed to help people switch attention from one thing to another. For people who have OCD, their cingulate gyrus doesn't forge connections with other brain areas as effectively as it could, and it finds it particularly difficult to switch away from intrusive thoughts. It's a bit like you're watching TV, and whenever a frightening image comes onto the screen the TV freezes. You try to use the remote control to change the channel or to switch off the TV: you even pull the TV's plug out from the wall, but nothing works! The image stays whatever you do! If things get really bad you get sucked into the TV and you begin to live inside the frightening image. Everyone around you carries on as normal while you're banging on the inside of the screen desperate to get out, but nobody understands what it's like for you. It's something like trying to wake up from a nightmare. It's the very high level of fear that comes with these thoughts that leads most people with OCD to get caught up in routines and compulsions. If they can find something that makes their intrusive thoughts feel less real, and it works, then of course there're going to do it!

Like me, most OCD sufferers I've come across, tend to struggle for years without having a clear understanding of what it is they're experiencing.

So here's my story of OCD, how I learnt to understand it, live with it, and ultimately, how I got it to work for me.

Chapter 1

The context

I will begin my story when I was 10. That's how old I was when I first noticed things changing in my brain. At the time I was living with my parents, my brother Paul, and my sister Marian, in a small three-bedroomed house in Sidcup, Kent, England. We lived in a close or a cul-de-sac as it was more formally known. The street had about 50 houses in it, all of which were small, near identical, semi-detached homes. Most people who lived on the street didn't have a car. Many of the children were younger than me, apart from Big Michael who lived over the road. He was about 14 and he didn't come out much. When he did he could become quite violent if games that we were playing didn't go his way.

Now, I couldn't claim to be whiter than white myself. I was a bit of a bully to my brother, Paul. Paul was three and a half years younger than me and we shared a room. He had a thick mop of ginger hair and a tendency to lose his temper from time-to-time. He was a little on the large side and quite heavily built. Most people recognised that if he lost his temper, it was a good idea to get out of his way. My mother often used to joke with my father that he was the milkman's son, because he looked so different to the rest of the family. My sister and I were quite cruel to him at times and regularly told him that he was adopted. He seemed to cope quite well with all the teasing. I guess being much younger he didn't really have any choice! I felt a bit uneasy about the way I treated Paul, because I knew that teasing wasn't right. But I teased him anyway. The truth is, it made me feel powerful. For example, there was the time when Paul was young and I convinced him to eat an ant, by telling him that ants tasted nice. After he ate the ant I then told him that he was going to have an ants' nest growing inside his stomach. I realised I had pushed my teasing too far when he started crying and ran to our mother for reassurance.

Paul also had a tendency to get himself ready in the morning while seemingly semi-conscious. It was as if he was still trying to finish off the last part of his sleep as he got ready. With his eyes half closed he would get dressed, eat his breakfast, comb his hair, and brush his teeth. My sister Marian and I used to think this was really funny, and wanted to show our babysitter what he did. So at the weekend we would wake him up 11 at night, turn on all of the lights downstairs and tell him that it was time to go to school. He would go through his automatic routine, get into his school clothes, pour out his cereal, and brush his hair. He seemed to fall for the joke every time, and was oblivious to the fact that the rest of us were still in our nightclothes. We did it more than once to the poor kid! When he finally woke up to what was going on he wasn't very happy.

One day, out of the blue, my mother asked to have a meeting with me. She sat me down and told me that she was going to be working full-time soon and that she needed my help. To a 10-year-old boy my mother's job sounded quite exciting. I knew very little about her work, except that she was employed by the Ministry of Defence. She couldn't talk about anything that she did, as it was all top secret. Later, I found out that she worked as a secretary in a building, 'on a floor that didn't exist'. The lift didn't even have a button for her floor. When she used the lift she had to go up to the next floor and then walk down a flight of stairs to get to her office. At that time it was the height of the Cold War, the Irish Republican Army were in full flow, and I think she probably had access to information that would have made her feel agitated at times. The position of threat to which the country was exposed kept changing all the time and each day she knew the threat level that the country faced: it was given to all staff as a colour. My mother was a worrier and constantly lived in fear that her office was going to be blown up one day.

At our meeting, my mother told me that I was to be given an extra level of responsibility. My job was to escort my brother and sister home from school and stay with them at the house until she got home at about 5.30. I was to be given extra pocket money specifically for doing this job. I felt very proud to have been given the extra responsibility and took it very seriously.

I counted down the days before I could carry out my new role, although I didn't give much thought to how I might actually do it. Unfortunately, when the time came to do my job, my parenting skills were truly awful and my brother and sister would never do what they were asked. I realised that I was totally outside my comfort zone. I wanted to follow the rules my mother gave me to the letter. My mother was petrified of us being abducted and continually told us never to get into a car with strangers, no matter how friendly people seemed. Marian and Paul were to come straight home from school. Once they got home they weren't allowed to go out, and they had to stay in the house.

When Marian and Paul didn't do what they were told, I used to hit them. I hit them for doing things like walking too slowly back from school; not doing the washing up; and for trying to go out to play in the street when they weren't allowed to. For me, everything had to be done right, otherwise I would fail in my job. I felt terribly conflicted and guilty about hitting them, but, as a 10-year-old, I told myself it must be OK as my parents regularly hit me when I did something wrong – which seemed like practically every day. That's what parents are supposed to do right? My brother and sister were rarely, if ever, hit by my parents. I think my father slapped my sister across the face once and it never happened again. Paul didn't get hit or punished because he never challenged my parents. To be fair, if he was involved in any wrong doing, I was usually with him, and it was probably my idea.

After doing 'the job' for a few days a type of farce began to develop. When my father got home from work my sister Marian would tell him that I'd hit her. She was only about 18 months younger than me and I don't think she liked me bossing her about. My father then used to hit me for hitting Marian. I would then get really upset about my father hitting me and would hit my sister for telling on me. My father would hit me again for hitting her. No one thought to sit down and talk about what was happening, so the same thing occurred over and over again. This was my life. I didn't know anything different! But, looking back, if I had been an adult, I'm sure that social workers would have removed Marian and Paul from me because I was unfit to look after them. My experience of the whole 'attempting to be a parent' situation left me feeling bad as a person.

When I wasn't doing my 'job' I spent most of my spare time playing out on the street. The younger kids looked up to me and I felt a sense of responsibility for them. One day, a young lad who must have been about seven or eight ran up to me laughing and said, 'Big Michael just showed me how to f**k down the woods.' I said, 'What happened?', 'We got our willies out and rubbed them together. We f****d! Yeah,' he said, as he continued laughing. Even though I knew nothing about sex back then, I knew what the young lad was telling me was wrong, and said, 'You shouldn't be doing that. You need to keep away from Big Michael!' In my mind I put up a red flag for Big Michael as someone to avoid as much as possible.

Many of the kids on the street were basically left to do whatever they wanted and led a feral type of existence. The twins down the road, who were about six years younger than me, only had one rule which was – There are no rules. They were smoking cigarettes by the age of seven, shoplifting sweets from the sweet shop, and getting up to all kinds of mischief. They broke into a local neighbour's back garden, took out the pornographic magazines from his shed, and kissed the pictures of naked women whilst in the middle of the street. I ran around after them desperately trying to get the magazines from them. It was quite funny, but I knew who would get the blame if they got caught. As they grew older I tried to talk them out of doing things like smoking and playing with fireworks, but they were basically unmanageable.

On one occasion my brother and I had a day off from our Catholic school. It was a day of 'holy obligation'. In Catholicism this meant that we were supposed to go to church to pray for a saint, although we never did. We used to spend a lot of our time in the local streams, getting into the sewers and places like that instead. This was where we lived: in the woods, in the fields, and in the brooks and streams. The previous day I had planned with Paul to travel through a large sewer pipe to see where it would lead. For us, this was an interesting adventure. We got our boots, a torch, and other things we might need. When the time came to go I said to my mother, 'We're just going down a tunnel!' She said 'OK. See you later.' She didn't ask for any further information, so in my mind what we'd planned was OK.

On our journey to the sewer we met the twins Rob and Chris, who must have been about four at the time. They asked if they could come with us. After a little bit of begging from them we told them they could come along. We approached the sewer entrance and one of the twins decided that he didn't want to come. We decided to leave him at the entrance, and told him that we would meet him there when we came out the other end. We travelled through this sewer, my brother Paul, the young twin Chris and myself. Eventually, about an hour or so later, we came out into a drainage ditch in a street a few hundred metres away.

On our journey back we saw Rob waiting at the entrance to the sewer. There were a lot of women gathered about chatting, but we thought nothing of it. Rob joined us, and as we walked back through the park that offered a shortcut home, we saw several men poking areas of the ground with pointy white sticks. I thought, 'that's interesting' and then forgot all about it. We continued walking and eventually found our way to another section of woods on the other side of our street. This area was called Beverly Woods. We played there for a few hours building a camp, until we got hungry, and it was time for us to go home. As we walked back down our street, rolling a large car tyre we'd found in the woods, we noticed two police cars blocking the street side by side with their emergency lights flashing. Apparently, the police were just about to inform our parents that we were missing, presumed dead! My mother was oblivious to the fact that the police were outside. I'm glad that we got home before the police told my mother the news, as she might have had a heart attack.

It turned out that, while waiting for us Rob had told a woman that his brother was stuck down the sewer. The woman then called the police. The woman didn't notice us walking past her and collecting Rob after we came out of the other end of the tunnel. Police divers were sent through the sewers and there was a huge search. We were told the search operation had cost £20,000, which 40 years ago would have been sufficient to purchase a small house in outer London. Apparently, the search operation was covered extensively in the local media, although I didn't see any of this myself. Luckily, I didn't get into trouble with my parents due to the fact that I had told my mother that I was going down a tunnel and that she told me it was alright. But I was asked by the police to write a letter of apology to the superintendent, which I promptly did. Basically, I felt a bit like a criminal at the young age of 10.

At school, things weren't the best they could be. My parents were strict Irish Catholics and they arranged for Marian, Paul, and I to attend a Catholic primary school called Our Lady of the Rosary. It was a small, friendly, and local state school, that was run by the Roman Catholic Church system. There were about 360 children in the school, aged between 5 and 11.

Our class had a teacher called Mr Blake. Looking back, he didn't have the best personality traits for a teacher. He would ask children to come up to the front of the class, tell them to bend over, and then hit them on their behind with a thick, black, lacquered wooden ruler that he kept on his desk. The punishment was two-fold: first, humiliation in front of your peers; second, physical pain. I can still see that thick wooden ruler on his desk right now. It's as clear as day.

There was something of a furore on one occasion as a girl in our class was given his punishment. A short while later, an edict was sent down from the headmaster telling us that girls could no longer receive corporal punishment. We were told that girls weren't allowed to be hit as it might affect them when they got older. In my mind I immediately calculated that this must mean us boys were immune from such things.

Mr Blake didn't believe in modern ideas like equal playing time for children in sports like football and cricket, and he didn't have much ability to relate to the children who he was teaching. As a result, he used fear to control and manipulate children in his classes. He also used praise on occasion. When Mr Blake praised you, you felt that you really must be great. His praise was very believable to a 10-year-old, but his wrath was even more convincing.

My time in Mr Blake's class felt like it went on forever compared to other classes. Looking back, I guess I must have been traumatised by it. I tried to change my behaviour to cope with my fear of Mr Blake and I remember I had started obsessing over my handwriting, attempting to make it as perfect as possible. I mainly concentrated on neatness, making sure that all my letters were written perfectly and that the spaces in between my words were exactly the same.

On one occasion we were asked to draw a profile of a face. A friend of mine, David Grace said it would be a good idea for the male face I was drawing to be smoking a cigarette. I drew this, and we laughed at it. I had no idea that I was doing something wrong. Mr Blake then called me to the front of the class and hit me with his ruler. This was the first time I'd ever been punished by a teacher. The pain from the ruler stung just a little, but the humiliation and shame was much worse than the physical pain. I was aware that my face was going red, I felt tearful, and was hugely embarrassed. If there was a kid that didn't need any kind of corporal punishment, that was me. Just being told off verbally was a source of great shame.

So that's the context of my life when I was 10. I was a little stressed by my environment, and I was clearly carrying too much responsibility for a 10-year-old. At home I had started ordering things like books by size and colour. I had also begun tidying and rearranging my room, which is very unusual behaviour for a young boy. At the time I didn't associate the strange things that had begun to happen in my mind with my environment.

Chapter 2

Blinking hell

On one occasion I was playing in the school playground when I came face to face with a boy a few years younger than me. He seemed different to the other children somehow. He appeared to have a problem with his eyes and he was making controlled and deliberate blinking movements with his eyelids. I asked myself: 'What must it be like for him doing that all of the time?' A little while later, after I had gone back to class, my attention was drawn to my eyes and I noticed that my eyelids had stopped blinking automatically. My eyes felt dry and for some reason I wasn't blinking. Waves of anxiety ran through my body as I asked myself, 'Why aren't my eyelids blinking: they should have blinked by now?' I felt that I needed to hurry my eyelids a bit so I made a deliberate blink. My eyes felt better immediately. I waited for the next blink, but it didn't come. My eyes had started to become dry and sore once more. I thought to myself, 'Somehow I've turned off my blinking'. I then felt that I needed to blink consciously and in a controlled manner. I didn't trust my eyelids to do their job any more, as they didn't seem to be blinking when they were supposed to. 'Was I now a 'blinker' just like the boy in the playground?' I started to panic. 'What if I've caught my problem with blinking from that young lad? Is this how it happens? If so, how can I fix it? What if I have this problem forever?' Thoughts like these ran alongside my controlled blinking for the rest of the day.

The next day I woke up and thought to myself, 'I wonder if this is going to be another day when I have this problem with blinking?' I immediately wished I hadn't asked that question as I again went into a pattern of controlled blinking. The same thing went on for a few days. I was beginning to get worried, but not worried enough to go to my mother with it. Luckily, the weekend soon came, and somehow I forgot all about my problem with controlled blinking. It just disappeared.

A number of weeks later, I bumped into the same boy in the playground once more. As before, I became fixated with his eyes and the way that he blinked. I immediately fell into a pattern of controlled blinking. I was in my classroom doing controlled blinking for about an hour or so, and asked myself, 'How did I get rid of this last time?' I thought back to when it had happened before and I recognised that I must have simply forgotten about it, because it just seemed to go away by itself. I realised that the more I focussed on blinking, the worse it got, so I figured that this must be part of the solution. I decided that what I needed to do was focus on something else and my problem with blinking would somehow go away. I immediately tried doing some work, which happened to be a range of puzzles that our new class teacher, Mrs Williams, had set for us. These puzzles were quite interesting and took a lot of mental focus, so I found that I was able to distract myself with them for a while. I noticed that my method of distraction was working in patches, and I felt waves of relief. But, every so often a worry about whether or not the problem with blinking was still there would pop into my mind. Each time I had this thought it drove me back to monitoring my eyelids and I found that I needed to do more controlled blinking. I persisted with distracting myself, while being bothered every so often by these intrusive thoughts until eventually it somehow clicked in my mind that my blinking would just take care of itself automatically if I didn't get involved. After about an hour or so I was able to let go of controlled blinking.

I recognised the problem was still around however. The boy in the playground was still there. I thought that if I avoided him, if I didn't let the thought of him come into my mind, or if I didn't look at him, then somehow it would be OK – that is, I wouldn't fall back into controlled blinking. But, from time to time while running around playing I would somehow bump into him, and there he was, right in front of my face, doing his blinking. Each time this happened it immediately brought my focus back to my own blinking. I then needed to follow the same routine of distraction, although I noticed the amount of time that I was doing controlled blinking for was getting shorter and shorter. As time progressed, I found that I could detach myself from controlled blinking in under a minute, so I became less and less anxious about the problem occurring. I went through a type of routine in my mind about just letting my blinking take care of itself, which was usually accompanied by a feeling of relief. If I met 'a blinker' I knew I could handle it. I felt that I had successfully dealt with the problem – or so I thought anyway. Back then, I didn't realise that once I had dealt with a problem like this, it would simply reinvent itself and come back as something else.

Chapter 3
The fortune teller

One day, I was playing a game called conkers in the school playground. If you haven't heard of conkers, a conker is a large roundish seed from a horse chestnut tree about an inch or two in size. To get a conker ready you make a little hole in the middle of the seed using a screw-driver, take out one of your shoelaces from your shoes, make a knot in one end of it, and then thread the other end through the middle of the seed. For us kids, after there was a windy day, finding horse chestnut seeds on the ground was like finding hidden gold. After getting our conkers ready, we would take it in turn to hit each others conkers until one person eventually won by breaking the other person's conker. I can't describe the intense satisfaction that we felt while playing this game. The winning conker would accumulate a score. The rule we had was that the winning conker would take on all of the winning scores of the losing conker. For example, if my conker was a 2 and I beat a 6, my conker would become an 8. We would all ask each other what score the other person's conker had before we decided whether or not we wanted to risk going into competition with them. My friend James Whitman had an amazing conker that was a 132. His dad had left it in a drawer for years and he had given it to him. It was as hard as a stone and James defeated everybody, until one day he left it in his pocket overnight and it became damp. After that he was devastated when his conker lost to Andrew Cunningham, who ran around the playground telling everybody who would listen. James looked crestfallen.

I was looking for a viable opponent to play conkers with when I met a young lad of the same age who was in a different class. He told me that he could read palms and asked me if he could look at mine. After a very short look he said casually, 'You're going to die young in a car accident!' and then walked off. After this the thought of dying in a car accident plagued me for the rest of the day. I rushed home and told my mother what had happened. I asked her, 'Am I going to die young in a car accident? Look at my hand!' My mother's response was something along the lines of, 'Don't be so silly. That boy doesn't know the future.' But to me what he said felt like an absolute certainty. In those days my father used to drink quite heavily at the weekend, then get into the family car, and drive us all home. He would use his knees to control the steering wheel while rolling himself a cigarette at the same time. Although these things weren't legal back then, many drivers did the same thing: the police generally overlooked traffic offences, and children weren't required to wear seatbelts. If I saw a car accident where someone died on the TV it used to fill me with horror. In my mind, dying in a car accident was the most frightening thing that could possibly happen to anyone. It seemed very real somehow. Of course, watching someone being shot or stabbed was perfectly reasonable!

As I got older I still experienced this intrusive thought of dying in a car crash. I was desperate to get rid of it. I looked up palmistry to try to reassure myself. I used to continuously check the lines on my hand. It had started to become a preoccupation. I began looking at my hands from different angles inspecting the lines up to 50 times a day, perhaps hoping the lines would change somehow. I kept focussing on one of the lines that I had read was called the life line. There was a slight gap in it. To reassure myself I told myself, 'Maybe the other hand is the real future? Perhaps it should have been the left hand that was read?' Different books said different things, adding more to my confusion.

When I was older, if anyone I was with suggested going to a palm reader or a fortune teller I would always refuse and walk the other way. I didn't want to be plagued with even more intrusive thoughts about the future. It was so hard to forget about that fortune teller even though he was only 10 years old.

Chapter 4

The ugly mug

On another day I was in the school playground talking with another lad in my year group called Paul Wallace. After talking with him for about five minutes, out of nowhere he suddenly said, 'You've got an ugly mug!' as he smiled at me. I'd never heard these words before. But he was smiling when he said it, so I thought that it couldn't be too bad. 'What's an ugly mug?' I asked. 'It means your face, Dumbo!' was his reply. I guess he wasn't the most tactful kind of kid. I couldn't make sense of it. 'What's a mug got to do with a face?' I thought. After that I didn't speak another word to Paul Wallace while I was at the school: I avoided him completely. A part of me felt deeply hurt to find that someone else thought I was ugly, and another part of me felt anxious that I might upset him with my face. I was a sensitive kind of kid and my reasoning was that I didn't want to hurt his feelings by showing him my face.

After that, the ugly mug comment stuck in my mind. I couldn't manage to shift it. Throughout the rest of the school day the thought of what Paul Wallace said was going round and round in my head: 'I've got an ugly mug! I've got an ugly mug! I've got an ugly mug!' After I came back from school, the first thing I said to my mother was, 'Paul Wallace told me I've got an ugly mug?' 'Don't be so silly,' she said, 'of course you haven't. You look fine! There's nothing wrong with you.'

My mother's suggestions didn't offer me much reassurance and I was still unable to detach from what I will now term this 'sticky' thought. The thought of having an ugly face and other people being unable to tell me about it started to become intrusive. Of course, other kids would have been able to ignore these thoughts, but to me they became stuck, going over and over in my mind. The thought didn't come to me that Paul Wallace had been going around telling half the kids he met in the playground that they had an ugly mug, or that he'd learnt it from his parents, who probably said it to him as a form of endearment. After all, he did say it in a nice way, smiling at me with his eyes when he said it.

Paul Wallace's comment wasn't the only thought that stuck in my mind about my appearance. At the time it was the late 1970s and my mother decided not to cut our hair, perhaps influenced by the Scottish music band The Bay City Rollers, who all grew their hair quite long. One day, I received a passing comment from a man who asked me whether I was a boy or girl. I then started to obsess over this. Comments like this would stick in my mind for years.

Chapter 5

I'm evil and I'm going to hell

Mr Jones was the deputy head at the school. Whenever I bumped into him, he always seemed friendly and engaging on a one-to-one basis, but for some reason that could only be known to him, he started to give us strange lectures before lunch that he termed 'grace'. Looking back, he was either going through some kind of personal crisis or he woke up on those mornings thinking, 'I hate kids and I hate my job!' 'I don't want to be here!' 'How many kids can I abuse at one time in the most effective manner?'

I remember two lectures that particularly affected me. In the first of his memorable talks Mr Jones explained to us in great detail how important it was to drink water with our lunch. He told us about all of the dreadful things that might happen if we didn't drink water and the serious impact of dehydration. The upshot for me was that we would die if we didn't drink water with our lunch. He then proceeded to tell us that we were not having water with our lunch that day because the previous day we had been too noisy. As soon as lunch was over, I rushed straight out to the playground to the water fountain. In my mind, there was going to be a massive queue, so I was surprised to see that there were only one or two kids waiting. I guess most of the other kids weren't as bothered as I was about about the very serious effects of dehydration!

In another of his famous lectures Mr Jones explained all about hell to us. He said that in the Catholic religion holy days of obligation were essential. He told us that if we didn't attend church on these days we would almost certainly go to hell. My heart started to race as I realised that I'd already missed a few of these church masses, and I was resigned to the fact that I must be going to hell. This idea got stuck in my mind and I couldn't get it out. I became so distressed about it that I kept asking my mother if I was going to hell. Her answer was the same every time and quite predictable: 'Whisht now' (which is Irish for 'be quiet')... 'You're not going to hell.' I didn't feel any sense of relief from hearing my mother's comments, so as a last resort I went to my father. For me to ask my father about such things was incredibly rare. His answer was very sensible. He told me that if I lived a generally good life I would go to heaven not to hell, and it was OK to make the odd mistake here and there as they didn't count. He then told me a saying that he would repeat many more times to me as a child: 'John Jones went to church every Sunday, but he went to hell for what he did on a Monday.' At the time I never quite understood what he meant, and kept asking him 'What did John Jones do on a Monday?' He kept saying, 'I don't know! That's not part of the joke!' I still firmly believed that I was going to hell.

Chapter 6

Burglars

Many children worry about burglars, but for me it became a fixation. Before moving to Sidcup when I was about seven or eight, my family lived in a part of south-east London called Grove Park. I think it's a nice place to live now, but back then it wasn't. My parents rented a large Victorian house and sub-let two parts of it to tenants. For my parents this was a way of making a little extra money to support the costs of bringing up a young family. I have memories of the house being huge, but in reality this was probably because I was so small. I remember that the house had high ceilings and felt very cold. There wasn't any central heating.

A big problem was that the house was burgled on a regular basis. In those days a common way to pay for gas was by using a coin meter that was topped up regularly with 50 pence pieces. Burglars seemed to learn quickly which houses had these coin meters, and would break into their cellars to target the meters. This caused a lot of disruption to people living in these properties because they were responsible for refunding the money to the gas board and repairing the locks if they were broken.

I wasn't aware of any burglaries at that time because I was too young, but once we had moved into our new house in Sidcup, my mother and father would often reminisce about how they were burgled. My father's favourite story was the time that burglars stole all of the money from their gas meter but hadn't noticed a pile of pound notes lying on open display.

My mother appeared to be particularly frightened of being burgled. On one occasion, one of our neighbours' houses in Sidcup was burgled while the family were away on holiday. My mother's reaction was as if someone in the family had died. She couldn't stop talking about it. This was the first burglary we'd heard about in the street. She couldn't believe that people would come into our quiet cul-de-sac in Sidcup and rob a young family. She became incredibly anxious about our house being burgled as well.

My mother's fear was transmitted to me and I became a little fixated on the subject of burglars. I began to have difficulties going to sleep at night. I would lie there with my eyes closed and all I could see were images of someone breaking into the house during the night. I rarely went to my parents with such thoughts because I already knew what they would say: 'Don't be so silly, there are no burglars coming.' I knew that my parents were downstairs, but the thoughts of burglars breaking into the house had a big effect on me. I made up all kinds of plans in my mind about how I might deal with a burglar coming into my room. My main idea was to pretend that I was asleep. This type of thinking didn't help me too much, however, as I also worried about my parents being safe.

It was then that I first became aware of a little voice in the back of my mind. It said, 'Just cross your arms over each other. This will create the shape of a cross and this will stop any burglars getting into the house.' I did this straight away as the voice seemed very convinced that this would work, and I found that I began to relax a little. I acknowledged that having my arms crossed over my chest did feel slightly uncomfortable, but it made me feel less frightened and worried, so I decided that the situation was bearable. I woke up the next morning and was a little concerned as I noticed that my arms were no longer crossed over my chest. But I was relieved to find that we hadn't been burgled during the night. I found that I started to do this arm crossing quite frequently at night: after a while, it became a routine.

Chapter 7

Was there something wrong with my brain?

Thinking back with my psychologist's hat on, I recognise that I was a very anxious and worried child. I lived with highly anxious parents. I had an overinflated sense of responsibility*, and at school I was taught by teachers who used fear to manipulate and control their pupils. But surely there were lots of other children aged 10 in exactly the same position as me? Why didn't all of these children go on to develop OCD as a teenager like I did?

When I thought about it, I did notice the start of changes when I was 10, but in reality I think my problems were set in motion much earlier. My mother told me that at a very young age my aunt Bridget had unofficially diagnosed me with Attention Deficit Disorder. My Aunt Bridget was a qualified nurse and one of my mother's older sisters. She was the brightest and most opinionated of my aunties. She was a very shrewd woman, well read, a fast talker, with a sharp mind. She had an opinion on everything. She was considered to be the posh person in our family. She had a sitting room in her house that could only be used on special occasions for important visitors, like priests, and she only read broadsheet newspapers – unlike my parents who read tabloids. Aunt Bridget's diagnosis turned out to be incredibly accurate. When I became a psychologist I found out using cognitive assessments that I had working memory difficulties. Working memory is an ability to hold and manipulate information in your mind at the same time, and problems with working memory are often associated with attention deficit problems.

My best guess is that I probably had problems with my brain architecture from a very young age. If you haven't heard the term 'brain architecture' before, it's a way that neurologists describe the development and growth of the brain. In many respects the brain is constructed in a similar way to a building. Experts suggest that the brain is the least developed part of our body when we are born. They say that if a baby's head were any larger it would struggle to move through its mother's birth canal. As a result, we are born with our brains not fully developed. After birth, the brain proceeds to construct itself from the bottom up, layer upon layer. The brain's outermost layer – the roof of the brain or the neo-cortex – doesn't finish growing in most of us until our mid-20s.

Looking back, I think that my brain was built on faulty foundations. Just like a building with poor foundations that falls down, or completely collapses when shaken by an earthquake, I started to experience mental health problems when I was faced with stress. I asked my mother about my early childhood and this reinforced my opinion that things probably did go wrong at an early age. My mother told me that when I was a small baby she secured a job in an accounts section of a large department store. As a result of this I was placed with my Aunty Jane during the day. My Aunty Jane and her husband Christy weren't bad people but, put it this way, they would be last on my list as potential childminders. As parents, they were very much at the top end of the negligence scale. To give you an idea of their parenting style I'd compare them to a tamer version of the Thénardiers in *Les **Misérables***. If you haven't read the book *Les **Misérables***, or watched the show or film, **the** Thénardiers were a family with whom **Fantine leaves her daughter Cosette. The** Thénardiers were rough innkeepers and although they were paid to look after Cosette, they treated her more like a slave. The major character Jean Valjean eventually rescues Cosette and brings her up as his adopted daughter after her mother Fantine dies. While I wasn't treated like a slave, my Uncle Christy frightened me, as he always seemed to be talking about some kind of scam to make extra money.

When I was a little older I got a chance to look around my aunt and uncle's house: which was also a pub. The best way to explain what I saw is to ask you to visualise a health and safety expert's worst nightmare. Wires from electrical appliances were stuck straight into electric sockets with the assistance of match sticks. There were no such things as electrical fuses or plugs. Pots and pans were embedded with grease and burnt food. Clothes were dirty and unwashed. Beds were unmade. There was one item in the bathroom that might have resembled a very dirty old toothbrush that all the family seemed to share. Alcohol seemed to be my aunt and uncle's major source of sustenance. These people were my carers when I was a baby. My mother told me that as a baby I came back from their house covered in lice. She said that she attempted to deal with this lice infestation by placing my head in a bowl of disinfectant. I was also apparently frequently given a dummy dipped in sugar and honey. This led to the quick decay of my baby teeth.

At home, it appeared that I also had a few close shaves. On one occasion my mother left me unattended in the bathroom, and she found me holding onto a half-drunk bottle of disinfectant. I was then rushed to the local hospital to have my stomach pumped out. I think I was also dropped on my head on another occasion.

Looking back, I think that this type of early environment probably could have had some kind of impact on my developing brain, or at least it wouldn't have helped. Research has found that prolonged stress in animals affects the development of a part of the brain called the pre-frontal cortex. This is an essential part of the brain for psychological wellness in humans. It has many important functions. It quietens down noise in the mind and it can call off emotional reactions. We also use this part of our brain to think about our thinking and to bring choices into conscious awareness. In later chapters I will describe a little more about how this part of the brain is affected by stress.

* Many people with OCD have what is termed an over-inflated sense of responsibility. This generally involves taking on responsibility for life factors that are outside the individual's control. Rule-based thinking patterns such as, 'If anything goes wrong, it's all my fault' and, 'If everyone is happy with me at all times, then I will be OK' are quiet common. An over-inflated sense of responsibility becomes especially apparent to some individuals when they find themselves in team and family environments. Many people with OCD tend to have excessive concern for how others feel, and will try to be in control of factors that are outside of their control. As a child I would often try to include other children who I thought were being left out. I would become very concerned about other children messing about in lessons: if they were making the teacher's life difficult. In any team game, I would burn myself out to help the team as much as possible. If I felt that I didn't have enough ability to help a team I was playing with, I would leave the team. If there was a last piece of cake I would always let someone else have it. If I was asked to help any old person with their gardening, I would always do it. I wouldn't ever have a party as a child because I didn't like the idea of anyone

not being invited and feeling sad about it. I didn't ask girls out on a date, just in case I might want to break up with them. I couldn't bear the thought of hurting other people's feelings. If I heard that my parents were struggling with money, I would ask for Christmas presents that cost little, and I would bring home any money my mother had given me for school trips.

Chapter 8

OCD grows with you

By the time that I became a teenager my problems had grown worse. All the themes that I'd struggled with as a 10-year-old had developed or become more sophisticated. By now, I was experiencing new intrusive thoughts and had symptoms of full-blown OCD: repetitive behaviours, avoidance, and several neutralising routines.

Looking back, as my brain was developing so was my OCD. Everything I knew, it also knew. It had access to all of my sub-conscious thoughts and fears. It could harness all of my brain's architecture, so it was as clever as me. If I were playing it at a hand of cards, it was as if it could see all of my cards. If I spotted something that was causing me too much distress, I tried to challenge it. But every time I thought that I'd won, it reinvented itself as something new. It was like playing chess with myself. Every move that I made, it came up with a counter-move that I hadn't anticipated. Each time, I thought I was dealing with a new challenge, but in reality I was dealing with the same opponent all along. It could read my mind and I couldn't hide anything from it.

Chapter 9

'You've done well, but you're still stupid!'

At the age of 11 I started grammar school. Looking back, I'm not sure what my motivations were for joining the school. The school's educational philosophy seemed highly elitist, and looking back this wasn't an ideal fit for me. On our first day new students congregated together to hear a talk by the deputy head-master, Mr Johnson. Mr Johnson began by introducing himself, and then gave an impassioned endorsement of the school. Following this, he said to the assembled students: 'You are the elite! You are in the top one percent of the population.' He didn't tell us what we were in the top one per cent of, but he did tell us about the huge expectations that the school had for its students. Mr Johnson told us what the school wanted from us when we became adults. A big focus was on how many students the school had helped gain entry to universities such as Oxford and Cambridge, and how many international rugby players it had produced. We were told that the school had come second in the country for results in terms of academic performance. This wasn't idle talk. I noticed as I walked into the assembly area, panel after panel of Oxbridge students' names written in gold letters on wooden boards in the school's main foyer. There were also framed and signed England international rugby shirts given by former students.

At the end of Mr Johnson's speech the students were separated into six houses. The process wasn't dissimilar to what happened in *Harry Potter and the Philosopher's*

Stone, although students' houses weren't selected by the 'sorting hat'. I was placed in a house called Williams, named after a former teacher.

I found that once I was in a class environment, students were ranked in terms of how they performed in each subject area. In each class you were given a rank between 1 and 30, with 30 being the lowest. This was one way in which the school encouraged open competition between students.

I remember finding it very difficult to pay attention in class. My mind would often zone out. On many occasions, I would wake up halfway through a lesson and realise that I didn't know what had been discussed. When I got home and it was time to do my homework I didn't understand what I was supposed to be doing, so I tried to complete it without comprehending the instructions. As a psychologist, I later found out that what had been happening to me with my zoning out was called dissociation. Dissociation is a detachment from reality rather than a separation from reality. Dissociation can work a bit like a fuse blowing in your mind when you start feeling too anxious. It's like a bubble goes around you and you feel disconnected from your environment and what's going on. Essentially, you know where you are, but your mind goes somewhere else. To other people it seems as if the lights are on but there's no one home.

I came second to last in my class at the end of my first school year, with an overall rank of 29. I was saved from being in last place by a student called John Proctor who had performed even more poorly than me.

In the following year at the age of 12, I was placed in a class with the dysfunctional kids and the kids who worked very hard but weren't as smart as the others. There was a distinct hierarchy at the school and it was generally recognised amongst our year group that our class, 2i, was one of the bottom classes. I didn't realise it at the time, but selection to the school was based on children having a high Intelligence Quotient (IQ). This meant that even the kids in the bottom classes had high levels of intelligence.

In our class we had six or seven kids with behavioural problems. One of them was called John Smith. At the age of 12, his hair was already greying. He was constantly getting into fights with people. He claimed that experts told his parents that he had a photographic memory. As a child I thought that he didn't seem to use it very much as he constantly forgot his lunch money, sports kit, books and all kinds of other stuff. I lost count of the number of times he asked to borrow things: money for his lunch, PE shorts, socks or a top. The last I heard, things hadn't turned out too well for him. I was told that when he was 16 he had attempted to rob his local jewellers by tunnelling in through their roof. I am not sure whether or not this really happened.

It was difficult to concentrate in this class as there were several kids like John Smith, all with attentional problems. I continued with my daydreaming or dissociating. Luckily, in class I sat next to Jonathon Harvey who was one of the harder working kids. When my attention was brought back to the room after dissociating I immediately recognised that I didn't know what was happening. I would ask Jonathon if I could copy a question, or if he could tell me what was going on. He was very helpful to me and highly tolerant. I felt grateful that I was sitting next to him. He was a bit like a personal teaching assistant to me.

The top dog in our class was David Brown. To me our relationship was a bit of a cliché. I was the oddball drop-out compared to his most-popular-kid-in-school type. David lived a typical middle-class lifestyle. He was very confident in his opinions; he was an excellent football player and rugby player; he dated the prettiest girl at school; and he was also very hard working. He liked to be the best at everything and he was used to coming first in the class. David was born to be a leader.

Although I liked David, he sometimes used to frustrate me because he often dismissed my suggestions. His usual comment was that what I was saying couldn't possibly be correct, because I was stupid. To be fair to him, he wasn't alone in this thought. Most of my classmates thought the same and these responses were coming from the kids in the bottom class! Looking back I can understand their reasons. I was zoned out half the time, and I was therefore never quite sure what was going on. I didn't do my homework properly as I rarely listened to instruction when it was handed out. My main focus was on going home to watch TV.

But then, near to the end of my second school year, something extraordinary happened. I was approached by the head of our year and he told me that I was going to be presented with an award for endeavour at the end of the year. 'Endeavour... What does that mean?' I asked, 'It means that we've noticed that you've been working very hard,' he said, '... and, we think that you've done well.' I was confused because I didn't feel that I was working hard. But I didn't want to hurt his feelings by challenging his thinking on the matter, so I kept my thoughts to myself. Looking back, the award was probably for efforts in other areas of school life rather than academic achievement, but I wasn't told this at the time. I worked exceptionally hard at sport and at any team game, due to my very high levels of perceived responsibility. I'm not saying that I won rugby games for our house team single-handed but put it this way, I gave everything and didn't allow other players in teams we were playing against to gain one try or point against us, tackling them whenever they got the ball. Our house team were outright undefeated rugby winners for four years on the trot. On occasions the team used to clap and applaud me at the end of games. This was a real honour and it left me with a great feeling. The same thing happened in cross-country running races. I ran much harder and I gave everything if I felt that my team needed me.

But this endeavour award rattled me, mainly because I struggled to make sense of it. The teachers had noticed me. I now felt a sense of responsibility to them. I felt guilty and unsettled as I knew I hadn't been working very hard at school. I had become used to the idea that I was stupid, and I felt a bit immune to the teasing from other kids, although it wasn't very pleasant. I also felt under a great deal of pressure, because I knew that other children like Jonathon Harvey had worked much harder than me in class. Then suddenly, out of nowhere, I felt as though a light bulb had switched on in my mind. I could resolve my thoughts about being stupid and ease my guilt at receiving an unwarranted award all in one go by working hard at school in the following year. This is the first time that I can remember channelling my obsessive thinking into something that could become vaguely useful.

The following school year seemed to come around very quickly, and I was still in a class with the same students.

The only difference now was that our class was called 3i. I started getting up at 6 in the morning to do school work. After school I went to the local library to complete further work. David Brown's voice echoed in my ears: 'You're stupid", 'Stupid, stupid, stupid'. These words seemed much worse coming from him because in many respects he was such a reasonable person. Proving him wrong became my main motivational force. The real issue for me wasn't actually being stupid: it was about me not being socially accepted, and others thinking that my ideas were worthless because I was stupid.

Within a year I had used my obsessive behaviour to work excessively and to get to the top or near to the top of my class in all subject areas, through coursework and exams. My maths teacher asked me to stand up and announced in front of the whole class that in the end-of-year school maths exams, my scores were on par with the scores of the top-performing kids in the school's top classes. I had gone from zero to hero!

I think my maths teacher was as shocked as I was when she saw my results, as here she was teaching a class for the less bright and dysfunctional kids. Then, finally the day came when our form teacher put a list of our overall class ranks on the wall. All students were placed in order from first to last, taking into account their combined scores from class positions in all subject areas. This kind of thing wouldn't happen now because it is so clearly abusive and divisive. Being top dog David Brown was the first to look at the results. His head lowered as he saw evidence for what he thought might have been coming. I had knocked him off his perch. I was now the form's prize-winning student.

The funniest thing about the whole episode was David's reaction at the end. In shock, while looking at his position on the list just below mine, he said, 'Yes, you beat me' – shaking his head – 'You did well. You might be good at school work … But you're still stupid!' After that, I gave up studying obsessively as my obsessions switched to other things, and I slowly sank back down the rankings once more.

Chapter 10

The mark of the beast

When I wasn't obsessing about other things, my thoughts dwelled on an idea that I was evil. By the time I was 15, I rarely did anything wrong. I didn't swear, I didn't smoke like many of the other kids, I didn't shoplift, and I discouraged any behaviour that might break the rules. I did a few experiments with animals that I seriously regretted, like the time I tried to wash the cat with washing-up liquid. The cat didn't like it and managed to escape with the washing-up liquid still attached. She got into quite a state when she tried to lick it off. Luckily my mother was able to clean her.

A regular intrusive thought that I had was that somewhere on my body I had the mark of the devil, and it was the number 666. This would explain to me why I felt so evil – a negative self-belief that I was fused to at the time. The intrusive thought of having a mark gave me a deep sense of unease. I thought that the mark of the beast could be a scar and it could be under my hair, so I often looked for it there.

One day as I was obsessing about my face I noticed what I thought looked like some very faint claw marks. In my mind the marks resembled the number 666. I became obsessed with these marks and felt compelled to check them from many different positions. I looked at them in mirrors where there was different lighting so that I could get every possible perspective on my face but they were still there. There were three fine lines that had a slight curve at the end.

Eventually, I got so worked up about them that I went to my mother. Holding my breath, I said, 'I think I've got the mark of the devil', and showed her the marks. She gave her usual reply which was something along the lines of, 'Don't be so silly, there's nothing there.' I said, 'Maybe the light's not too good here, I'll show you upstairs!' She refused, giving the excuse that she was busy, but these very slight lines were there. I wasn't making it up! Luckily, later that day I discovered what in fact had happened to my face to make the faint marks. When I was a baby my mother had dropped me, and in her desperate attempts to save me she had caught me with her nails, scratching my face. Sure enough, the very faint scar looked very much like finger nail marks. The next day the family video recorder was removed. My mother told me I was watching too many films that I shouldn't.

My intrusive thoughts then switched to another angle – that I might be possessed by an evil spirit. A full-blown vivid image entered my mind of me bursting into flames as I entered a church. Following this, I started to avoid going to church with my family: at times that I did have to go, I waited outside in the lobby area. My thoughts were incredibly vivid and felt real. One day I thought to myself, 'I've got to challenge this. I can't go on like this any more'. Also a girl who I liked was sitting in the church and the pain of my avoidance was beginning to hurt more than my intrusive thoughts. So hesitantly, I walked in. I immediately noticed that nothing was happening, so I continued walking, sat down, held my breath, and waited to burst into flames. I was incredibly frightened, but unsurprisingly the flames never came. After this I lost my fear of going into the church and wondered how I could possibly have believed such a thing. But my intrusive thoughts then adjusted their angle. My thoughts told me that being in the church was OK, but if I blessed myself with holy water that it would burn me. At that time I felt that I could get by without holy water, so gave it a miss for a couple of years until I eventually tried it and of course nothing happened.

But, my intrusive thoughts didn't stop there. As I grew into an older teenager I started to become plagued with thoughts that somehow I could be responsible for the deaths of others. The people who might die were not specific and neither were the numbers. The uneasy feeling I got I interpreted to mean that the numbers of people were very high. I heard a quiet voice in my head telling me that I could resolve this issue. It said, 'Just go up and down the stairs, but you must make sure you do it properly. If you do it right you can cancel out the deaths.' So there I was going up and down the stairs. I got into a pattern of missing the first step and making sure that I only trod on every second step. When I got to the top of the stairs I wasn't sure if I had done it right, so I felt a compulsion to continue doing it. I kept doing it over and over until I felt much less guilty and anxious.

I continued carrying out my stairs behaviour for a while and things stabilised, although I was spending quite a bit of time on it. But then my intrusive thoughts began pushing things to a new level. A thought told me that one person was definitely going to die. I could pick the person. It would either be a good friend or my grandfather. I knew whatever I chose would be wrong. My intrusive thoughts had me cornered. The voice that recommended what I should do to cancel things out was strangely quiet. I felt extremely agitated.

With no escape from the intrusive thought, I felt I couldn't do anything else except challenge it. 'Do what you want!' I said to it; 'I'm not getting involved in this decision making process anymore. Whatever happens, happens, you decide, but I'm not playing your game any more!' The same intrusive thought kept returning for a while, and each time I maintained my position saying the same thing over and over a bit like a broken record. I started to believe that I was winning, as the intrusive thought felt a little weaker each time I challenged it.

To take things even further I dropped my stairs habit completely. I even trod on a stair that I wasn't supposed to. I then found that I was able to leave my compulsion with the stairs behind to some extent. Interestingly, if I return to my parents' house I recognise that the memory is still there. It's a bit like the stairs are saying to me, 'I'm still here. You know you can come back to me whenever you want to.'

Chapter 11

I am overrun by germs

As a teenager I found out what germs looked like. I'm not sure if I saw a programme about them on TV, or if I saw a picture of them in a book, but the thought of germs terrified me. I started experiencing intrusive images about them. In my imagination these disgusting little creatures were crawling all over my hands. I didn't connect them to making me ill or being sick: it was just the thought of them being there and crawling over me that left me feeling unsettled.

As soon as I had these types of thoughts I would immediately go and wash my hands. I then started to think about how these creatures could get onto me, from door knobs and touching things. As soon as I had one of these thoughts I went straight to the bathroom to wash my hands. I was in and out of the bathroom like a yoyo. My parents didn't say anything. I think they must have thought something like – 'He's strange; just say nothing and let him get on with it!'

Luckily, this was a short-lived compulsive episode which I challenged with psycho-education. I found out that hands are covered with friendly bacteria, which look equally disturbing, and that bad bacteria fight for space on the hands with good bacteria. I came to a position in my mind that bacteria was everywhere and I would just have to ignore it. My intrusive thoughts in this area then began to subside and I dropped my compulsive hand-washing behaviour.

Chapter 12

My body's faulty

As a teenager I spent a lot of time at our local Catholic parish social club. The club was set inside the grounds of the local church and was dedicated for the use of the church's parishioners. The inside of the club was stained with cigarette smoke and stank of stale beer. The club was a hive of activity and it was the centre of my parents' social life. They could talk with their friends, play darts and pool, and drink cheap beer. Unlike in public houses in England, children were allowed into the club. My father always looked forward to going to the club and he took us with him.

The club became a basis for most of the fun we had in our lives, although in reality it was no more than a large prefabricated hut. Our friends congregated there to socialise. The club was only open Thursday to Sunday and we went there whenever it was open. There was an ethos at the club that alcohol was something that you drank only at the weekend. Like many of the other teenagers at the club I was gradually introduced to drinking beer.

One day I needed to visit the male restroom. A shared urinal ran the length of the wall and I took my position in between two men. I waited to go, but nothing would come out. I felt highly embarrassed and felt a rush of blood to my cheeks. Nothing was happening. All I could think was, 'Are they noticing that things aren't working? Perhaps they think you've come here to look at their penises?' I did up my zip and returned to the main area of the club, but I still needed to visit the restroom. I went back a few more times and still nothing would happen. It had become an issue. Eventually, a cubicle became available and I used that instead. Things worked much better in the cubicle. Following this, the problem occurred so many times that I felt as if it was playing a game with me and I became unable to use public urinals for quite some time.

The bus was also a place where my body's potential reactions tormented me. I had a fear that I would lose control of my penis in public. I first noticed it when I was sitting over a wheel on a bus. It was something about the vibration and the movement. But the more I focused on trying to stop it happening the worse it got. Sweat was dripping off my forehead as I started to panic. I had nothing to cover myself with. In my mind young women were looking at me, noticing what was happening. I tried to keep my mind blank, but this didn't seem to be helping.

After that I kept having intrusive thoughts about it happening again when I was on the bus. I avoided sitting on seats over wheels. But there it was: my genital area throbbing as the bus went up and down. I focussed on it, trying to control it. I didn't have any sexual thoughts, but just like my blinking before, I had lost trust in that part of my body. Back then, I didn't realise that focussing on it would make it worse.

When I wasn't on the bus my intrusive thoughts switched position to other things. I started becoming preoccupied that women would think I was looking at their breasts. If I was talking to a girl or a woman I used to keep my gaze up. I kept saying to myself, 'Just focus on her face'. But then, every so often, I would catch myself noticing breasts. I would then experience waves of embarrassment. It was as if I was in a constant battle with myself.

If I wasn't worried about losing control of various body parts I was focused on my health. My mother was very anxious about health, and worried about us getting cancer. She would often say to one of us, 'Is that a lump?' and then start anxiously inspecting a part of our body. We felt sorry for her at the time, because she was so clearly distressed about nothing and we used to make fun of her for thinking such things. Interestingly, I didn't think it was funny when I became pre-occupied with my own irrational thoughts. During one period, for some reason, I lost trust in my heart and went through prolonged periods of checking it. An internal voice told me that if I monitored my heart I would remain alive. I didn't know how to check my pulse back then so I would place my hand on my chest to make sure that I could feel regular vibrations.

I must have been 13 or 14 when one day I felt that I had no heartbeat. I went running to my Aunt Anne who was a nurse, saying, 'I'm dying! My heart's not beating!' She was the first person with whom I shared my private fears with about my heart. She knew about the body and how the heart worked. For some reason, whatever she said struck a chord with me and my obsession with checking my heart disappeared for a number of years. It felt like such a relief to let it go at the time.

Chapter 13

You're so vain!

A problem that I had been obsessed with ever since my 'ugly mug' fixation was my appearance. As I grew into a teenager I began to focus even more on my facial features, and in particular a small mole on my chin. I had intrusive thoughts that I was ugly, and a thought that my face wasn't symmetrical kept popping into my mind. By the age of 14 I became so fixated on my hair that I was combing it hundreds of times per day. I was checking my hair from hundreds of different angles and looking at it in different mirrors. I was often hours late for things because of this obsessive checking. I got into a pattern of holding onto my hair to help it stay in a particular position. At the back of my mind I knew that when I went out my hair would move about: but when I got into this repetitive loop it was really hard to break away from it. Of course many teenagers do this: it's just that I took it to extreme levels.

After a while, I recognised that continuously looking in mirrors was making me feel flat and miserable, so I decided that I wouldn't look in a mirror for a week. It was initially difficult to achieve, but I proceeded to avoid all mirrors. As was my nature back then, I did this in an obsessive way, covering up mirrors in the house and trying not to catch my reflection in shop windows. Although I was obsessively avoiding my reflection, I recognised that my mood had, in fact, started to improve. I started to feel more of a connection with others and inside felt that I had turned some kind of a corner. In retrospect, I probably felt better because I was reducing my self-focus and I was spending more time attending to others. This meant that I could forget about myself for a while at least.

As I grew into an older teenager my intrusive thoughts changed their angle to me being vain. My thoughts also suggested that if just one person thought I was ugly, then I was ugly, as this cancelled out the opinions of anyone who told me that I was good looking.

On one occasion at a party I was smiling at a girl called Olivia Paggit who I had taken a shine to. She was standing with another girl and two boys who may have been friends or boyfriends. One of the boys said in a mocking voice, 'You're so...ooh good-looking', laughing at me in a high-pitched ridiculing manner. He was probably unaware of how his words cut through me like a knife. There could be no way that he would know how my thoughts tortured me, and punished me to such an extent that I didn't want to live any more. He was right – I was vain, but I had the side of vanity that meant I had excessive concern about my appearance, and I also had an extreme fear that other people would think I was vain. He had me in check-mate!

After hearing the young man's comments I was so taken back that I didn't quite know what to say, so I just smiled and walked away. All I could really think was, 'He knows'. This was at a felt sense level rather than anything that made sense logically. His mocking voice got stuck in my head, going round and round non-stop. I thought to myself, 'They know that I'm vain and he said it. Olivia Paggit was smiling so this means that she agrees with him.' I thought she wouldn't want to go out with someone who was so shallow and ridiculous. I went into a full-scale relapse. I went straight to the bathroom mirror to look at myself. I spent about an hour or so looking at my face from different angles, inspecting it and trying to rearrange my hair. Essentially, I was trying to soothe myself but nothing much seemed to be working. I felt so empty that I just wanted to die.

Looking back, it's hard not to feel sorry for myself as a teenage lad with all of these insecurities. The irony was that I liked that girl, and although I wasn't sure, I felt a vibe from her that she might have liked me as well. I felt so insecure about my appearance that I would never have asked her out on a date. This was despite what anybody said to the contrary.

Chapter 14

OCD and limerence

In the *Oxford English Dictionary* limerence is defined as a 'state of being infatuated or obsessed with another person, typically experienced involuntarily and characterized by a strong desire for reciprocation of one's feelings but not primarily for a sexual relationship'. Limerence was first used in 1979 by the American Psychologist, Dorothy Tennov in her book *Love and Limerence*. Tennov spend years researching the concept of romantic love, reading thousands of written testimonies, before refining her ideas.

Although I'm quite happy using the term limerence, I'll need to let you know that it is not fully embraced by many psychologists, who prefer to view obsessive love as a disruption within a normal attachment process. It wasn't until I became a psychologist that I discovered that OCD sufferers are especially prone to suffering from it. My experiences of limerence weren't dissimilar to what happens to those poor monkeys who have electrodes inserted into the sub-cortical parts of their brains. They feel a compulsion to stimulate their pleasure pathways over and over again by pressing a lever. It's hard to detach from anything when you are obsessive, and it's incredibly difficult to separate the self from limerence.

Rozina Farugia wasn't the first object of my limerence, but she was certainly the most painful. When my limerence for her was at its peak I felt exhilaration after spending the smallest amount of time with her – even having a cup of tea with her resulted in euphoria. I wasn't unlike people with addictions who I've listened to talking about crack cocaine. The ups of being around her felt incredible, but they were equally matched with the unbearable depths of despair of being away from her. Boy, it was painful! It was as if there was a direct link to euphoria in my head and Rozina could press it over and over again whenever she wanted. A smile from her, a look from her, spending the shortest amount of time with her, and going to lunch with her created waves of exhilaration. I felt trapped by it. I knew there was something seriously wrong with me, but I felt a compulsion to continue what I was doing anyway.

I first met Rozina, through my work at a branch of Lloyds Bank in London when I was 18. I had known her for about a year or so before my limerent feelings started. Rozina was a beautiful young woman from Malta. Five years older than me at 23, she was petite, with a soft shade of olive skin, beautiful brown eyes, and long curly hair. She was married, slightly unhappily it seemed, (although I could never be fully sure) – to her husband Jeff, who was an engineer. I think Rozina didn't get much attention from her husband at home, and possibly, due to her insecurity, she had a tendency to flirt with the young men around her. She had a desire to be found attractive, and she needed it reinforced on a regular basis.

Early on at the bank, Rozina had singled me out for some flirtatious attention. Although I wasn't as psychologically minded back then as I am now, it was quite easy to recognise that flirtation was a type of harmless game for her, as she moved her attention from one person to another. I found it difficult to know exactly how to respond to her as Rozina was married. I decided it was best to minimise any game playing with her and to keep as much distance as possible. I didn't feel any physical attraction to her, although I recognised that she was a beautiful woman.

My limerence for Rozina started after we got to know each other quite well by chance. Due to building work being carried out at the bank, we were placed together on our own with very little work to do for a few days. Our job was to be key holders, to keep an eye on the bank vault, and to make sure that the builders didn't go into any bank areas that they weren't supposed to. Our situation meant that we had time to kill, so we talked a lot. Our chats developed our friendship and as time progressed, we chose to work with each other more often. Rozina began to disclose more and more information about her life: her thoughts, her deepest fears, and her indiscretions. I found what Rozina had to say fascinating. I was an avid listener, and after a short amount of time I felt as though I knew practically everything about her, including her deepest secrets.

After a while I began to feel desperate to spend time with her. This created a state of conflict within me as Rozina was a married woman. Internally, different aspects of myself argued between themselves. Ultimately, I was able to justify to myself that spending time with her was OK as long as it was work-related socialising: so it was OK to go to lunch with her, or go for a drink after work with her, as long as others came too. Occasionally we went out on our own, but I tried to avoid that where possible. After a while other staff members had begun to whisper about our relationship and on a number of occasions I was approached by senior bank staff and asked directly if Rozina and I were having an affair. An affair would be against bank rules for security reasons – two colleagues working together could quite easily clear out the contents of a bank safe, or transfer large amounts of money. I was shocked and immediately denied it, but could see how others might have thought that it could be the case. I began to worry that my feelings for her were too obvious.

I tried to deal with the problem by spending much more time with single women at the bank and spending less time with Rozina. I kept what had been said to myself, and didn't tell Rozina about what had been happening because I felt ashamed. Telling Rozina about what had been said might have required being open about my feelings, and I didn't want to do that.

My friends tried to help me out by setting up potential dates with attractive women, but I passed up these opportunities in order to stay fused to my limerent love. I couldn't detach myself emotionally from Rozina. I loved her in an obsessive way. I knew there was something wrong with the way I felt, and that it was infatuation, but I felt powerless to stop it nevertheless. I was like one of those flies that get drawn into a fly-trap and then don't know how to escape from it. What I was getting from the trap was a type of nectar that was gradually killing me inside. I didn't know what limerence was back then, just like I didn't know what OCD or being obsessive was, but I knew for certain that it made me feel miserable. Thinking about it this way, it's so easy to see how limerence is referred to in the literature as love's unhappy cousin.

As I began to distance myself from Rozina, she started to flirt with other young male bank staff once more. I recognised that it was something she needed to do. Feeling physically attractive and wanted assisted her with her underlying insecurity, and compensated for a lack of attention from her husband. But it was tearing me apart. I couldn't stop looking at her. What was she doing? Where was she going? Who was she looking at? I became jealous of Rozina giving attention to other male members of staff and this confused me. I didn't want to feel jealous! I didn't want to have a physical relationship with Rozina! I didn't fantasise about her sexually. My obsession with her was purely romantic. But I couldn't bear the thought of letting go of her emotionally. I continuously reminded myself that she was married, that she wasn't mine, and therefore I couldn't lose her. This didn't stop my obsession. I thought that I loved her, but the thought of attempting to take things any further went completely against my value system. I also knew that Rozina's flirtation with myself and others was due to her own insecurity. I felt very guilty about my feelings, but I couldn't stop thinking about her. My thoughts about her haunted me. I turned to drinking large amounts of alcohol every day to block my feelings and I started to become desperately unhappy.

Eventually, I found that I could no longer tolerate the intensity of the feeling that I was experiencing on a daily basis. I was thinking about Rozina practically every moment of my day, but was unable to do anything about it. I decided to write a letter of notice to the bank. I didn't have another job lined up. I was prepared to throw away a secure job, with good prospects because I couldn't bear the pain of limerence anymore. Although I loved Rozina, I knew it wasn't a healthy type of love. My love for her wasn't a love designed to be shared with her. It was an obsessive kind of love that was really all about me. This is the true nature of limerence – it is, after all, as song writers might say, 'a selfish kind of love!'

Chapter 15

Thoughts about those teenage years

Looking back on my early and mid-teenage years it seems as if OCD was my constant companion. I didn't have a clue that all of the different problems I was battling with were part of the same thing.

Like many people who are prone to OCD, my symptoms increased during significant periods of change. Physically, I was a late developer. Others around me were maturing and developing faster than me. I was left behind in the growth stakes. By the time I was 15, most of my peers were more than a foot taller than me. Many boys in lower years than me at school were also much taller than me. There were about four of us late developers left in the year. We all knew who the others were, but we didn't discuss it with each other. We were viewed as immature by our peers. For me, maturation was a difficult and uncertain time.

I have learnt over the years that OCD creates a distraction from real-life issues, and it's highly likely that instead of worrying about my lack of development I became totally caught up in my obsessions. For people who have OCD their minds struggle to shift position, and accommodating change is very difficult. There is also an urgency to stay with what you're doing, or to stay with what you know, even when the product is quite useless or the behaviour is harmful. My obsessive behaviour probably contributed to my experience of depression which I began to develop when I was about

15 or 16 – one in two people with OCD go on to experience depression. OCD thinking and behavioural patterns can place a huge amount of stress on the brain. Higher cortisol levels, possibly brought about by a stressful life, tends to result in lower serotonin levels (Dinan, 1994). When supplies of serotonin run low our brain cells begin to lose their ability to communicate with each other, or they 'lose their voice' and people experience symptoms of depression. Symptoms of depression can include low mood, reduced or increased appetite, lack of interest in usual activities, poor concentration, increased or reduced sleep, reduced sexual activity, feelings of hopelessness, lack of energy, increased pain perception, thoughts of suicide, feelings of worthlessness, feelings of not being able to function, feeling slowed down, and increased irritation.

My symptoms of depression were also connected to my shame of being a late developer. I couldn't compete at sport like I used to. In rugby I was a boy playing against men and I couldn't impose my strength on others like I had when I was younger. Looking like a child at the age of 17 was very difficult to deal with emotionally.

Luckily, in about the space of a year, between the ages of 17 and 18, my growth accelerated. My father was constantly measuring me before and throughout this time. By the time I was 18 I had grown to 6ft 2. My father didn't say anything, but he must have given an internal sigh of relief that I had finally grown.

Chapter 16

Dark years

My symptoms of depression continued well into my adult years. As a result of memory problems often associated with depression, my life between the ages of 20 and 30 is still quite foggy and hazy in my mind. These years weren't dominated so much by obsessional thoughts and behaviour but by dark thoughts. It was as if the volume button on my intrusive thoughts was turned down somewhat. I was numb and switched off at an emotional level. My experience wasn't dissimilar to the zoning out that I had as a child, but it lasted for years rather than the 20 or 30 minutes it used to. Perhaps I had driven my brain so hard over the previous decades that it had switched off somehow.

Between the ages of 20 and 30 I had so many jobs that I've lost count of them all. I experienced interpersonal problems and was sacked from my employment on quite a few occasions. As time progressed, I found that my CV was beginning to look less and less promising as I moved from one job in finance to another. On paper, I thought I had begun to look unemployable: out of desperation, I began working for financial companies with dubious or unethical outlooks. These companies turned out to be a very poor fit for me, so I gave up working in the City.

Following this, I continued to work my way down the pay-scale hierarchy. Eventually the only work I could find was temporary work in factories, delivering pizza, and working as a cleaner for minimum-wage. A friend of mine Joe, a fund manager at Hill Samuel (a leading merchant bank in London at the time) tried to call me and left messages with my parents over a period of several months. I didn't return his calls. I treated him very poorly considering we had developed a close friendship over a number of years. I basically abandoned him with no thought about how it might affect him.

Moving from plush offices to factories was a bit of a culture shock for me and I was dismissed from two of my minimum-wage cleaning jobs for not following instructions as requested. I am embarrassed to admit that practically the only job I didn't get the sack from before I was 28 was my pizza delivery job at Pizza Hut, and even that job was painful sometimes. On occasions, I found myself delivering pizza to some of my by now successful grammar school peers, who appeared speechless when they opened their door to find me standing there with a pizza for them.

By that time my sense of inadequacy was fully reinforced and I had switched off emotionally. I became quite hard-up financially and my mind-set had become extreme and rigid. I didn't want to use the unemployment system or to ask my parents for help, as in my mind this would have confirmed to me that I really was not succeeding in life. Sometimes I couldn't earn enough money to pay rent, so I ended up spending months living in a tent at a campsite where the rent was £4 per day. At other times I could pay the rent but was left eating potatoes and baked beans as my only source of nourishment.

I continuously felt that I was failing in some way. I felt empty inside. I just didn't feel like I had the energy to do things; I wanted to escape from my problems and myself. The only time I really felt OK was when I was asleep. I became quite avoidant and more nocturnal. I often didn't attend events that I had been invited to, mostly without sending an apology or letting people know. I didn't answer the phone to friends or return their calls. The number of friends I had dwindled to just one. I think the only way that this friend managed to tolerate me was to laugh about the way I behaved, and to recognise that my behaviour was not about him. My self-esteem was so low that I genuinely believed other people wouldn't notice or care whether I turned up late for planned events, or would even be bothered if I attended them at all. *All my focus was on myself.* It was a pitiful kind of self-loathing with endless questioning about why my life was so broken. I was so detached that I had little regard for other people's feelings or my own. Most of the time I didn't want to live anymore and hoped I would die. It was as if my body, mind, and personality, were unacceptable to me.

Chapter 17

A change for the better

By the time that I reached my late 20s I knew I had to do something to change my life, but I wasn't sure what or how. After much thought I decided to enrol on an undergraduate degree in psychology. I'd had an interest in the mind ever since my mother first made an appointment for me to see a hypnotist as a teenager. Like many people, my mother thought that if I could be hypnotised, then maybe I could be made normal in some way. I still remember the hypnotist's house. It was quite literally a mansion. His house doubled as an old people's home, and there were always a few friendly old people sitting in the waiting area who said hello.

The hypnotist definitely had a way about him. He had a pointed beard and looked dramatic, as if he had just walked off stage. He taught me about the unconscious mind and how it worked. Following our meetings I used the techniques he taught me to work on my unconscious mind. I found that it helped in patches.

My psychology degree was my saviour. I met my life partner there, Nicola, who was almost as obsessive as me. A little while after starting my degree it felt as if I had begun to wake up. Nicola helped me a lot with her in-depth knowledge of psychology and I found the ideas that we discussed fascinating. The part of me that had been so obsessed all those years ago suddenly switched itself back on to super drive. I became fixated with psychology. I felt OK about being fixated, because at least this was an obsession that I actually seemed to enjoy and found pleasurable. I still had intrusive thoughts, but they remained contained within one theme: my health. I had regular intrusive thoughts that I had; contracted HIV from my dentist; contracted a neuro-degenerative disease from eating a beef burger 10 years earlier; heart disease and cancer. The list was endless. As I gained new knowledge about illness my intrusive thoughts had more information to challenge me with. But interestingly, my intrusive thoughts seemed dimmer somehow, as if they had lost quite a lot of their power. A really important factor was learning what they were and what kept them going. It was a bit like having a noisy radio on in the background, which eventually I was able to get so used to that I didn't hear it anymore. Occasionally, I would find myself listening to my intrusive thoughts, but then I would realise what I was doing and bring my attention back to other things. Instead, I chose to obsess about my degree. I felt that if I had something that I could really fixate on, frightening intrusive thoughts would leave me alone.

As was my nature I approached my degree in an obsessive manner. I used a mini version of the approach used by Sir David Brailsford, the chief coach of the British cycling team. If you haven't heard of David Brailsford, he created a revolution in British cycling by using an approach called marginal gains. Using a marginal gains approach you spend less time focussing on the final result and instead break down all the factors that are involved in excellent performance to the smallest individual parts. A focus is then made on improving each small part. For cycling, Brailsford focussed on thousands of little things such as the type of paint used on a bike, the weight of a bike, and the posture of a cyclist. His theory was that although each small gain would be viewed as insignificant by itself to the final result, the accumulation of hundreds or thousands of marginal gains would end up being significant. Brailsford was right: he moved British cycling from being international also-rans on the world stage to achieving complete dominance of the sport.

Being obsessive, I broke down my degree into its minutiae and focused on refining each area of study, no matter how small. I did things like changing my diet to improve my concentration. I found that eating protein meals led to me being able to concentrate for longer periods. After I had finished studying I would then eat carbohydrates to provide the energy for my mind the next day. I learnt that the most successful students worked in teams, so I found the most intelligent students to team up with. I accessed the most difficult to find research papers. I used meditation and other methods to stimulate creativity. I didn't drink alcohol. I worked longer and harder than most of the other students. I also worked through the night on projects as I couldn't detach from them. If there was any area that I thought could lead to improvement I accessed it. I did get distracted and pulled off course by a few obsessive problems, which I would now class as danger areas, but while I was obsessing over my studies I didn't have the time or resources to fully get pulled into other areas of obsession. My obsession had a focus. My degree became my all-consuming passion and fixation. It was a bit like all those years ago when I was 12 obsessing over my school work. But at least I had something that I could obsess over that wasn't painful.

In my third year of my undergraduate degree I realised that I didn't want my obsession with psychology to stop. I'd heard about the field of clinical psychology, but at the time I didn't grasp how difficult a career it was to get into. To save you looking it up, clinical psychology is defined in Wikipedia as 'An integration of science, theory and clinical knowledge for the purpose of understanding, preventing, and relieving psychologically based distress or dysfunction and to promote subjective well-being and personal developments.' Lecturers on our undergraduate course told us that we shouldn't even consider a career in it as we would be wasting our time. I decided that I wasn't going to believe my lecturers, so getting onto a doctorate course became my next fixation.

I found out that to get onto a doctorate course I needed to be employed as an assistant psychologist for at least a year. But when I started applying for jobs, I realised what the undergraduate lecturers had meant. There were more than a 100 applications for each assistant psychologist position. My first-class degree which I had obsessed about for three years seemed to count for nothing, and nor did my one year of clinical experience as a nursing assistant on acute and secure mental health wards. I couldn't even get an interview for an assistant post. I received rejection letter after rejection letter. I realised I would need to find a different way to stand out in a sea of highly driven young graduates, many of whom were from England's elite universities, including Oxford and Cambridge.

Being obsessive, I enrolled myself on three therapy training courses at the same time as I thought that this would give me an extra edge. I decided on Mindfulness training at Addenbrooke's Hospital in Cambridge; a two-year postgraduate degree in Counselling

Psychology; and a one-year diploma in Parks Inner Child Therapy (PICT). Two of the courses required you to have therapy at the same time as your training. In reality, I had reached the heights of insanity by even thinking about doing all of these courses at the same time. But, at an unconscious level, therapy was what I really needed.

Chapter 18

Data gets an emotion chip

The first therapy course that I attended was the PICT course. The PICT course taught a version of a therapeutic process called transactional analysis (TA). TA was designed by the Canadian Psychiatrist Dr. Eric Berne in the 1950s to help psychoanalysis become more accessible to the general population. Instead of using terms, such as id, ego, and super-ego, common in psycho-analysis, he used terms such as the child, the adult, and the parent within. In his best-selling book, *The Games People Play*, Berne developed these ideas further, demonstrating how different ego states – self states – interact within and between individuals. Berne's ideas became fundamental to me: an exploration of self-states would later become a basis for my doctorate and my solution for OCD.

The essence of the PICT training was to develop different aspects of the self, mainly the child, the adult, and the parent within. Trainees on the course were therapists of some kind already. An exemption had been made for me to attend the course as my partner Nicola had suggested to Penny Parks, the founder of the training, that I had the necessary therapeutic skills to attend. Nicola knew Penny Parks personally, so Penny agreed to let me come onto the course.

At the end of our first day, trainees were asked to give open feedback to each other. I was shocked by what the other trainees said about me. The rest of the group were women and the upshot was that they felt as if they were working with a robot. Essentially, they said that when they worked with me they got a feeling that they were talking with a machine. I mumbled something nice back about them, but I wasn't able to think straight because I was in a state of shock. The lady who had started the 'robot' feedback had travelled all the way from Northern Ireland to attend the course. She was such a gentle young woman, and she told me what she thought in such a kind way that I had no choice but to take her comments on board. I hadn't realised that therapists could be so ruthless, direct, and to the point, but could be so nice at the same time!

A machine! ... No emotions! Was this really the case? The idea of being a robot got stuck in my mind and I started to get fused to it. Was I really like a machine? I guess I pushed myself as if I were a machine. When I became obsessed with something, I pushed myself longer and harder than anyone else I knew. I didn't appear to have a button marked 'stop'. At the time I did nothing for myself in terms of hobbies. Any extra time I had, I tended to channel into whatever I was obsessed about. Back then, I also didn't realise how suggestible I was. Any type of perceived negative comment could get locked into my mind. It was just like all those years earlier when Paul Wallace said that I had an 'ugly mug'.

I then began to obsess about the idea that I didn't have feelings. Maybe I didn't have empathy for others? How could I possibly work therapeutically with people without empathy? Was being a therapist a poor career choice for a robot? Had I made the wrong decision in trying to be a psychologist? I felt confused. I didn't want to be a machine. Looking back, I didn't realise that, like so many other people who were obsessive I spent practically all of my time in analytical mode, thinking, and being in my head. While I did this I tended to lose complete awareness of what was happening in my body. This was what the other therapists were picking up on when they gave me feedback.

As the course continued I was still obsessed with the idea that I didn't have feelings. I knew that I would really struggle to be a psychologist if I didn't address the feeling side of my nature. The main tool that I had used to gain success in my degree, my obsessiveness, definitely wasn't going to work on this therapy course.

As we continued our training we worked on each other, exchanging roles as client and therapist. Penny Parks the founder of PICT, was our guide. Here I was, totally outside my comfort zone, feeling completely de-skilled. While I was working with others, thoughts were rotating around my mind like, 'If I am a robot, how do robots cope with things?' and 'Can robots really love?'

I wasn't unlike the character Data in *Star Trek: The Next Generation*. If you haven't seen *Star Trek*, Data is one of the crew members of the starship Enterprise. He is a chief science officer, and a sentient, humanoid robot who operates from a purely logical perspective. He's fixated on the nuances of humanity. A lot of the human behaviour that he observes makes absolutely no sense to him. What is the purpose of love? Why do people get angry when they don't really have a right to? What makes people behave self-destructively? Data didn't need to sleep so he worked on his human project while others slept. A need for recreation puzzled him. To be frank, the similarities between Data and myself were quite eerie. Yet I could console myself because, despite being a robot, Data's interest, curiosity, self-sacrifice, and care for humanity, made him one of the most endearing and, ironically, most compassionate characters in *Star Trek*.

In one episode, Data creates an emotion chip to make himself more like the humans who he constantly tries to understand. This chip allows Data to access all the emotions that the other characters have. After turning it on, Data starts to behave irrationally; he experiences mood swings; he falls in love; he experiences anger and jealously; he begins to put his own emotional needs ahead of the group's interests. By the end of the episode, his emotions have become so self-destructive that he decides to remove his emotion chip. Watching this episode had a profound effect on me. I could connect with what had happened to Data. I felt that I had switched off my emotion chip a long time ago for similar reasons.

To complete my therapeutic training I would need to turn on my emotion chip once more and this had the potential to create havoc in my seemingly ordered and mechanical mind. As our training progressed I worked harder and harder to connect with some of the areas that caused problems for me. The best way to describe what was going on in my head was that it was an outright civil war.

Some parts of my mind wanted things to stay exactly as they were; other parts desperately wanted change and progression. I tried to access vulnerability, and painful things that had happened to me in the past, but other parts of me denied access. At times I felt as if I was frozen. Painful thoughts were there in the background, but no words would come out. To gain access to even small areas of concern required a battle. There were a huge number of battles in this war.

Understanding and re-evaluating my childhood created a major crisis, especially when I discovered that I had learnt negative beliefs, such as 'I am bad' from my parents. The *Oxford Dictionary* definition of to believe is to 'Accept that (something) is true, especially without proof.' The essence behind PICT training was an idea that we are biologically pre-programed to accept a rapid transfer or download of both positive and negative belief-based information from our caregivers through our interactions. The most obvious ways that we develop limiting beliefs don't really need any scientific evidence or scientific explanation. If parents or caregivers tell their children that they are weak, stupid, worthless, or a failure it's purely logical that most children will develop limiting beliefs! Most of us would understand that children treated in this way would develop a negative view of themselves. I also learnt that children develop limiting beliefs through negative messages from care givers that are implied through action and inaction. I was taught that once a child develops limiting beliefs they are usually very difficult to shift and tend to be retained into adulthood. Indeed, recent research findings are beginning to back up these ideas. The suggestion is that at a most basic level, children can absorb their parents' fears through simple sensory processes such as smell: this can occur in the womb and up to the age of six months, (Debiec & Sullivan, 2014).

Based on the above ideas, what I thought were intrinsic parts of me, such as being bad, weak, a failure, unlovable, and worthless, I discovered were no more than an illusion.

The civil war continued. After the rebels made a breakthrough in one area, there was usually a huge kick-back by the conservatives – I am using the term conservatives to indicate the parts of me that wanted things to stay exactly as they were, and I'm using the term rebels to describe the parts of me that wanted progress and change. After particularly challenging therapy sessions I felt much more positive, and I began to believe very different things about myself. I felt that I was beginning to wake up from my robotic trance.

I also learnt about dissociation. I had been experiencing dissociation for much of my life, but didn't know what it was. I found out that dissociation can be triggered by seemingly harmless environmental cues that remind individuals of things that happened to them in their past. This can result in individuals continuously going off into dream-like trances and losing track of conversations. It suddenly clicked why people thought I was stupid when I was younger.

Coming home after training days I felt enthusiastic about my life, and I was ready to embrace change. After important 'change sessions' I tended to have very vivid dreams, although I cannot remember what they were about. But often the next day, things appeared worse. It was as if over-night the conservatives had regrouped and were making an all-out offensive to regain lost ground in an attempt to go back to the way that things were before. The battle was relentless. My obsessive behaviour began to take over big time. The house was immaculate. The garden was completely weeded. Flowers were planted. Furniture was restored and repaired. It was as if the obsessive part of me was desperate to create some kind of external order to compensate for my internal chaos. Change felt very frightening. But in the background I was aware that something was stirring. It seemed that while all this was going on a part of me that had been sleeping for years had begun to wake up from its stupor. It seemed to be watching, in its semi-awake state, observing what was going on and waiting patiently for the war to end, and for the obsessive part to wear itself out. It was like a leader that was watching a squabble going on, and was waiting to intervene when both sides had run out of energy and options. It would then come in and implement change.

The PICT diploma that I completed remains the most powerful therapeutic work that I engaged in in my life. Through the course, I began to find out about and develop this amazing concept called self-compassion. For the first time in my life I had began to care about, and even like myself for short periods. I began to do things for myself. I started taking care of my appearance. I exercised. I bought myself nice clothes. I gave myself time to complete a hobby. It was as if I had just come out of prison. A story that Penny Parks told me also resounded in my mind.

Penny told me that there was once a couple who regularly watched an antiques show called *The Antiques Road Show*, a television programme on the BBC in the UK. People bring their antiques onto it, evaluators tell people all about their objects, and then finally say what they're worth. Penny Parks said that this couple really wanted to be on the show, so they went through their house looking for the oldest thing they owned. Eventually, they decided to bring this huge vase onto the show. When it was the couples time to see the evaluator, he was really interested in the vase and started asking them all kinds of questions about it: 'How long have you owned this vase? Where did you get if from? Where do you keep it?' The couple patiently explained that it had been in the family for years, for as long as they could remember. They confessed that the vase hadn't been of much interest to them, and that they only brought it to the show because it was the oldest thing they thought they owned. When the evaluator asked the couple where they kept it, they said they kept it near their front door as it had been useful for visitors to store their wet umbrellas in. They also sometimes used it to prop open their front door. The evaluator was visibly staggered at what he heard and said: 'I need to tell you something about this vase. This vase is so rare that it is considered priceless.'

The couple's mouths dropped open in shock as they tried to register this. They quickly nodded in agreement as the evaluator told them that they needed to treat the vase very differently and to get it insured immediately. The couple walked away carrying the vase very differently than when they came onto the show. The vase had been priceless all along, it was just that the couple in their ignorance hadn't recognised its true value. Penny Parks then delivered the killer line: 'It's the same for you. Others might not have recognised your true value over the years and perhaps treat you poorly, but just like the vase you've been priceless all along!'

Hearing this story was like a bomb had been dropped on the conservatives. They were totally defeated in a matter of seconds, and it would take a long time for them to regroup. After hearing that story I made a firm resolution to myself. From that moment on, I was going to treat myself very differently.

Change didn't come easily for me, however: I still had many old habits to contend with. On one occasion I had some written work to do for my Counselling Psychology degree. In the back of my mind I thought to myself, 'It's OK, I can work on that through the night, just like I've done so many times before.' However, when I tried to work during the night I realised that something had changed. A part of my mind told me I needed to take care of myself. I needed to rest.

... 'REST'...

What was this! I hadn't experienced this before. The compassionate part of my mind had pulled the plug on what it considered self-abuse. The compassionate part of my mind required that I work very differently. It reminded me about the vase story. I was no longer allowed to work to the point of exhaustion. I had to learn to work on things spread over longer time periods. This required adjustments to the way that I worked. I needed to treat my work like a job and spread it out. I could work in a disciplined way, but then I had to stop. I could no longer push myself to the extremes I had previously. I was still extreme, just not as extreme.

As part of the process of therapy, I had started to become more switched on to emotions. Because of this, I also needed to take my feelings into account. Before this, I simply ignored my personal feelings. Relationships needed to be completely re-evaluated. Things that were OK before, were now no longer OK. This took others including my partner Nicola, some getting used to. The person who she'd first got into a relationship with wasn't the same person anymore. I had changed into a person who now thought much more of himself. This would be difficult for anybody to adjust to. It caused some arguments as I put boundaries around my new sense of worth, but over time we managed to settle into a new status quo.

Chapter 19

Strange things these thoughts and feelings

Four months after finishing my degree, and after dozens of rejection letters, I breathed a sigh of relief as I finally opened a letter inviting me for an interview for an assistant psychologist post. On my CV I'd been able to write down that I had completed a course in mindfulness, that I was more than half-way through a diploma in PICT, and that I had begun a postgraduate diploma in counselling psychology.

I had now found a key to getting interviews. Following this I had several interviews, but still was unsuccessful in securing a job. I then had a little luck. I was interviewed for an assistant post by two clinical psychologists, one of whom had been on the same Addenbrooke's mindfulness course as me. I caught a break due to our joint interest in mindfulness and I got the job. It also happened to be the case that employing an assistant psychologist who was also a counselling psychologist in training would look good for their psychology department. I could work on one-to-one therapy cases for them with clients who they considered less demanding.

This presented me with more problems, however. To help other people with their difficulties I really needed to have a good handle on my own problems. I still hadn't fully grasped how to relate to my own emotions. To help myself with this, I started to have my own cognitive behavioural therapy (CBT).

The main books that I'd read on CBT suggested that thoughts affected the way that you felt, and the way that you thought and felt affected the way that you behaved. Each psychiatric disorder seemed to have a different CBT model that explained how the disorder worked. A CBT model for panic was very different to a CBT model for depression. However, the main thing that all the CBT models seemed to have in common was that people's behaviour and how they reacted to their feelings tended to keep people's problems in place. The general idea behind CBT was to become aware of the cycles that you got caught up in. Once you knew that you were in a cycle you could make changes and then leave your mental health problems behind. For example, in a case of OCD a person often feels highly anxious about their intrusive thoughts and wants to neutralise them. A CBT therapist would explain to their client what was happening to them using diagrams on a whiteboard. The client would be educated about intrusive thoughts and informed that neutralising emotions by carrying out compulsive behaviours reinforces or strengthens their fear of intrusive thoughts. This, of course, results in problems being maintained. In my CBT there was a focus on learning a) how to react differently to my intrusive thoughts and b) how to reduce the amount of neutralising that I was carrying out. The full CBT process is much more complicated than this and a full explanation merits a whole book by itself. But the meaning I took away was that if I could make small changes and relate to my fear in a different way then I would feel much less anxious.

I wanted to discover much more about CBT, so using mindfulness techniques I'd learnt I started observing the contents of my mind. The first thing that I recognised was that thoughts came in many different forms.

Thoughts could be image-based, and the quality of the images could range from incredibly vivid to blurred and difficult to see. Thoughts could be full-blown or fragmented. Thoughts could be like a voice in my head, telling me to do things, or could even tell me off about the way that I did things. I recognised that many thoughts could carry meaning and that thoughts didn't necessarily always come in the forms of words or images. I also became increasingly aware that thoughts rarely stayed in my mind for more than a second, unless I dwelled on them.

The more I listened to my thoughts, the more I recognised that different parts of my brain were talking to each other. As I studied neuropsychology I began to identify thoughts that might come from different brain areas, and this increased my curiosity even further.

One day I laughed to myself as I listened to the contents of my mind. As a poorly paid assistant psychologist I didn't have the money to complete do-it-yourself (DIY) projects properly. I couldn't afford to pay the fees of tradespeople, to buy the correct tools, or to buy the right materials. As a result I was endearingly nicknamed Mr Bodgit by my partner Nicola. I would set about doing DIY jobs that relied mainly on using the conceptual part of my mind. (The conceptual part of the mind is mainly used to solve non-verbal problems and is based in the right side of the brain.) Tasks might be mounting a TV to a wall, restoring furniture, or putting a wardrobe together from scratch. I tended to problem-solve as I went along and I would make an occasional mistake or two. On one occasion I could hear the verbal part of my mind (which is mainly based in the brain's left side in men) saying something like, 'You're an idiot, you shouldn't have done that.' This then triggered another part of my mind, which said, 'You shouldn't be talking to yourself this way, it's not going to help!' I noticed that this type of thought was somewhat like a manager or a parent. Here I was trying to do this task with this conversation going on in my head.

I reasoned that the managing or parenting type thoughts must be coming from the pre-frontal cortex, as this is where I'd learnt in my training that we tend to think about thinking. I observed how the managing part of the mind listened to other thoughts. At times it agreed with them, and at other times it overruled them. It would say things like 'I know you want to finish that off, but we're going to take a break for lunch'; 'I know you'd like to eat that ice cream, but do you really need it? I've changed my mind, go on then, you may as well have it this time!'; 'I know you'd like to stick with what you want, but sometimes it's important to be flexible'; 'Let's stand back from this'; 'Is what you're doing really necessary? How does it fit into the big picture?'

I learnt that thoughts that direct other thoughts are known by cognitive therapists as 'meta-thoughts'. I also recognised that there were a multitude of thoughts and that most thoughts were well behaved and patient. Most thoughts came to awareness in an orderly fashion. They tended to get on with each other like a team and each thought knew its position. They were very different to the intrusive thoughts that I mentioned earlier, which felt much more like bullies.

Chapter 19
The worst kind of bully

If you walk into the OCD unit of Bethlem Hospital, in Beckenham, England, you'll see a monstrous life-size figure created by the renowned sculptor Steve Caplin. This figure was commissioned by consultant psychiatrist David Veale, an expert on OCD, on the suggestion of his patients. The figure somewhat resembles a metal demon. It has a horrific snarling face, horns, and has metal scissors and knives stuck into it. The figure is holding a large Perspex tube into which people can place anything that maintains their obsessions. Lots of CBT experts suggest the best way to challenge OCD is to externalise it – to view it as outside themselves. If OCD could be viewed as a frightening bully it could then be challenged. I couldn't fully grasp why OCD was a bully, so I started to think long and hard about it.

I thought about the types of bullies that I had personally faced in my childhood and classed them into different levels.

Level one bully

I determined that a level one bully would be physically intimidating, without offering additional aggravating emotional content. Essentially, bullies like this might push you around a bit, but didn't frighten you psychologically. I decided that Steve Brightman, a young lad from my old school, would fit the bill for a level one bully. He was physically strong, and he was the toughest kid in our school year. I got into a fight with him once in the middle of one of our judo lessons. The fight happened after the judo instructor left the room to run an errand and told us not to do any judo while he was gone. I guess Brightman felt a need to challenge the authority of the judo teacher and immediately called me over and told me I had to have a fight with him using jujitsu, a Japanese martial art often used for close-quarter fighting in the military. Although initially hesitant, I was encouraged by the other children and I felt obliged to fight. Over the years I had tried to build a reputation among the other kids as someone who had no fear to compensate for my deep-seated anxiety that I was weak. Once the fight started I realised right away that Brightman was stronger than me, but I had the better technique, which meant the fight would go in my favour. I wasn't frightened of Brightman and viewed our fight like a game. It turned out to be quite an easy fight and after about five minutes Brightman conceded.

As I regained my composure I realised that I had made a terrible mistake. The other kids stood there open-mouthed in shock. There were mutterings of 'Manning just beat Brightman'. No one knew quite how to react. I had broken the school hierarchy. Everything had changed. Things weren't safe any more. I realised I had got carried away with the fight without thinking of the wider implications. Would the other kids now think that I was the toughest kid in the year – the top dog? Urgent whispers started to grow louder. A stream of thoughts hit my mind very quickly. An image came into my mind of a queue of unknown kids waiting to take me on. I imagined Brightman waiting for me later outside the school, accompanied by his hard gang, which included most of the dysfunctional kids in the year. My biggest fear wasn't the fights; it was the unknown and getting into trouble with the teachers. I also had a fear that I was bad and because of this I was petrified of being told off by the teachers.

My fear of being bad was far stronger than my fear of being weak, so a minute later I had already decided on my plan. I would ask Brightman for an immediate rematch, and help him to regain his mantle of being the hardest kid in the year. The status quo would be restored. Everyone would feel safe once more.

I said, 'Steve, let's have a rematch.' I had already decided that in the rematch I wouldn't offer any type of resistance. When the fight started, Brightman came flying at me like a man possessed. He threw me over his shoulder, as he was pretty useless at using good technique. I landed badly on my shoulder, partly dislocating it. I conceded and the fight was over in less than a minute. I felt relieved. Although I was injured I didn't need to worry about being the toughest kid in the year any more, although the shoulder problem would stay with me for the rest of my life as a reminder.

Level two bully

I decided to class a level two bully as physically intimidating with an added emotional component. David Finch would fit the bill here. He was in the year above me at a neighbouring school, and he had a reputation as a violent bully by kids in our neighbourhood. He had a sense of menace about him, so you turned and walked the other way if you saw him coming. Kids at our school viewed him as a psychopath who needed to be avoided at all costs. I was told that if he got into a fight with you and beat you that he would rip your school blazer in half. It was as if he was taking a scalp after a victory.

David Finch would sometimes walk through our street as if patrolling his territory. If we saw him coming we would usually go inside. He didn't pick on anyone in particular, so there was a sense of togetherness among the kids on the street. We'd heard that the father of a boy in our street had gone around to David Finch's parents to complain about his behaviour, and that David Finch's father punched the boy's father in the face. I don't think I need to say any more about what we were dealing with!

One day David Finch came down our street. Our house was locked as my mother had gone to the shops and we couldn't get inside. He cornered me outside my house, and started pushing me, the younger kids, my sister, and the girl across the street around. David Finch and I got into a fight. As we started fighting I felt fear for my life and thought, 'My God, help me, I'm fighting David Finch!' Our fight turned into a wrestling match as the other kids looked on. When it came to the fight I felt I needed to put everything into it. I strained every muscle in my body. It was life and death as far as I was concerned. I wasn't just fighting for myself but the security of the street, which gave me additional strength. Luckily, I just about matched David Finch for strength as I had worked for quite a while as my father's labourer and I was full of adrenalin. I put all my focus into physically restraining him, putting him into a headlock and using judo and wrestling strategies that I'd learnt. I didn't want to hurt him so focussed on wearing him out. He had huge amounts of strength – I immediately recognised that he was the strongest person that I'd ever fought. He was much stronger than my Irish cousins who I'd had years of play-fighting with.

Luckily, after about 10 minutes or so, David Finch and I both got tired and we decided to end the fight. As we got up off the ground he declared himself the winner and so did I. In effect the fight was a draw – we were both too tired to have another fight to decide the winner.

David Finch came back down the street again, but he didn't seem quite so frightening any more. The other kids and I ganged up on him and started to push him around, taking his belongings and throwing them into a tree. The feral twins and their older brother joined in and David Finch retreated to a house that no one lived in. He sat on the house step, looking forlorn and tearful, holding a brick in his raised hand, trying to make sense of his new situation. I guess we had started to bully him.

Level three bully

Steve Brightman and David Finch were nothing like the next bully that I bumped into. Although I'd had scrapes with them, I didn't feel emotionally terrorised by them. After having a fight with them I could walk past them in the street without any problem – they didn't really bother me any more. For me, though, a level three bully had the ability to strike emotional terror to such an extent that it made you feel physically and mentally unwell.

I met a level three bully one day as I was walking down a road called Willersley Avenue, which was near to my house. Willersley Avenue was a tree-lined, picturesque road, with large set-back chalet-type houses. Extra lawn areas had been laid to create even more of a barrier between the pavement and the street. It really was a beautiful avenue.

As I turned a corner of Willersley Avenue to walk towards my street, I started to relax as I was nearly home. I was in a dreamlike state when all of a sudden I was startled by a push on my shoulder. A teenage lad stood in front of me, staring at me intensely. He was about a year or so older than me, with curly brown hair and a freckled face. He looked slightly angelic in appearance. 'You beat up my little kid brother,' he said, prodding me with his finger.

I was rattled. What he was saying made me feel highly anxious. I wasn't in the habit of beating up 'little kid brothers' and I couldn't recall having beaten up anybody. He couldn't have been talking about Steve Brightman, and he didn't look big enough to be David Finch's older brother, although it might have been a possibility. I immediately said, 'No! I didn't beat anyone up! Who is your brother? I think you're getting me confused with someone else!'

'You don't need to worry about that!', he said. 'He told me all about it. I know it was you who did it! I'm going to get you! Not today... But I am going to get you!'

After that, the thought of the teenage lad continuously intruded into my mind. My thoughts tortured me and I dreaded walking home from school. My total focus at that point was when was he going to come and 'get me' and how I could avoid him. I wasn't worried about him physically hurting me; it was the idea that somehow he thought I was a bad person, that he could come and 'get me' any time he wanted, and that I had absolutely no control over when and if it was going to happen.

I thought about ways I could avoid him. I kept changing my route to and from school, and I continuously changed the times I walked home. When my mother asked me to go with her to buy a new coat, I jumped at the chance and asked for a parka jacket. The benefit of a parka was that it had fake fur around the hood. You could draw the hood together using a drawstring and conceal much of your face. I thought I could hide my face with this coat while on the way home from school so the bully wouldn't recognise me. Interestingly, looking back, I didn't think about him getting me at any other time. Back then, I thought he would only 'get me' on my way home from school because that was when I met him initially.

In my mind my strategy was working, as a good six months or so had passed without any further contact with the bully. Then one day, when I had practically forgotten about him, I had just got off a bus when I heard the sound of running footsteps coming in my direction. I felt a sense of dread when I felt that familiar shove to my shoulder and heard his voice, which I immediately recognised. I felt as though I was stuck to the floor. He said, 'Did you think I'd forgotten about you. I'm still going to get you!' My heart began racing violently. 'You just wait. It's not going to be today, but I'm still coming for you!'

I was a bit like one of those big dogs that don't realise how strong they are cowering in response to a smaller, more vicious, dog. In my mind he was much bigger than me (although physically he was only slightly bigger) and he had all of the power – after all, I had given it to him. Although I didn't ever hear from him again, it took another year or so for me to forget about him. He was able to produce a huge amount of fear in me in just two interactions without making any real physical contact. My journeys home from school had felt excruciatingly painful for at least 18 months. Looking back, who knows how many other young people he did the same thing to? The thought didn't come into my mind back then.

For me, the third bully was by far the worst. The most painful part of the experience was living in fear. So thinking about bullies this way I understood what David Veale meant. In many respects my intrusive thoughts were like the worst kind of bully – a level three. I couldn't stand up to them, because I never knew where they were, or when they were going to intrude into my mind. Like the bully, my intrusive thoughts made threats, but never carried them out. I guess if the threats had been carried out it would have been difficult, but I would have dealt with them just like I did with Steve Brightman and David Finch. They would then have lost their hold over me.

Thinking psychologically, intrusive thoughts were even worse than the third type of bully, more like a 3++. Whatever was triggering my intrusive thoughts had access to all of my thoughts and memories. It knew everything that I knew, and it could delve into my unconscious thoughts as well. As I mentioned earlier, it had access to all of my cognitive hardware so it was as clever as me. To compete against it felt impossible.

Chapter 20

Is OCD like a protection racket?

Thinking of my OCD being like a bully still left me feeling a bit confused. Surely, I thought, the 'helpful' little voice that told me what I could do to make things go away was on my side and was very different to the intrusive thoughts bully. But then it suddenly hit me! It finally registered in my mind that having OCD was like being drawn into an old-fashioned protection racket. If you haven't heard of a protection racket I will explain how it works.

To set up a protection racket, a gangster employs trouble-makers to rough up a neighbourhood's shopkeepers, and generally cause mischief. After a while, the shopkeepers don't feel safe any more and start to feel traumatised. The police aren't able to help the shopkeepers, as the trouble-makers always seem to be one step ahead of the law. The shopkeepers imagine their businesses failing and their lives going down the drain. Each shopkeeper wonders how he or she will remain in business if these problems continue.

A little while later a 'saviour' comes along to one of the shopkeepers. The saviour is friendly, smiling and well dressed, like a businessman. He says to the shopkeeper, 'I hear you've been having trouble with these thugs who've been harassing you. I think it's terrible that this is happening. These guys are a disgrace and I really want to sort these people out for you so they don't cause you any more difficulties with your business. What is happening to you is wrong.'

The businessman continues: 'I like you and I want to pay some people to take care of these thugs for you. This will be costly for me and it will be risky. I will also need to pay the police to turn a blind eye to what I'm going to do with these trouble-makers. Believe me, this is a dirty world that you don't want to get involved in! The less you know about it the better. You're much better off keeping out of it and doing what you do well, which is running your shop.'

The businessman then says, 'Now, I really hate to bring this up as it's a bit embarrassing, but I will incur a lot of expenses in protecting you so I will need to charge you. I'll try to make it as easy as possible for you. If you can pay me a small percentage of your income each week I can arrange for your shop to be protected. While you are under my protection you won't be bothered by thugs. I can make this problem go away for you. The good news is that you won't need to know anything about how I deal with this problem, so you'll be in the clear as far as the police are concerned.' The shopkeeper doesn't fully grasp at the time that the well-dressed man has actually paid the thugs to rough him up. Relieved, the shopkeeper agrees to pay a small percentage of his income to have protection.

As time progresses, the businessman returns a few more times and says it's costing a lot more money to keep the police quiet, so he needs to increase the rates. After a while, the shopkeeper struggles for money. The 'kind' businessman offers to lend the shopkeeper money at very short notice, but says that he needs to borrow that money from others at very high interest rates. He says that if the money isn't paid back on time the lenders won't be happy and they will probably burn down the shop or kill the shopkeeper's family. The shopkeeper thinks that the gangster is trying to help him and borrows the money.

The shopkeeper makes repayments for while, but before long, with the extra outgoings of the protection money and the interest on the loan, the shopkeeper eventually finds that he doesn't have the money to pay back the loan and is terrified. The shopkeeper goes to his 'saviour' for advice. The 'saviour' thinks long and hard about what to do and finally suggests that the only way to resolve the problem is to hand his business over to him and he will continue to make the repayments. The 'saviour' would then own the business and the shopkeeper would work for him at an hourly rate.

Relieved, the shopkeeper gives up his shop to the gangster, and he now works for the gangster. But, unknown to the shopkeeper the 'saviour' is not finished there. He tells the shopkeeper that he is having trouble making the payments from the business to the 'lender' himself and will now need to take things to a new level. The gangster tells the shopkeeper that he is going to arrange for an accidental fire in the shop, and that they will claim on the insurance. He tells the shopkeeper that he will need to be away on a certain day when this fire happens. He also tells the shopkeeper that he needs to borrow some money against the business from a bank and will need to take out a life insurance policy on the shopkeeper as this is what the bank requires. He tells the shopkeeper in passing that one of his associates likes his teenage daughter. At this time, the shopkeeper sees his life going up in smoke, and he is living in fear. He doesn't know how he got himself into this mess and he is desperate. It seems that the more the shopkeeper gives the gangster, the more the gangster wants.

I thought to myself, OCD works in exactly the same way. It generally starts off small and asks for very little. But the more you give it the more powerful it gets, and the more it wants!

I thought about that little voice when I was 10 that said, 'Just cross your arms over your chest.' It was as if it was saying, 'If you do what I say, I'll take care of you, and offer you protection. You don't need to know how I do it. I will protect you from bad things happening to you. Just pay the price by carrying out the neutralising behaviour I suggested. Surely it's not too much to ask. It will take just a little bit of your time.'

But after a while the little voice told me that the neutralising behaviours weren't enough to cancel things out or to stop things happening any more. It started asking for more and more. I kept giving and giving until after a while it felt bigger than me. Then, just like the shopkeeper, my OCD owned me and I was working for it. Even when it owned me, it still wasn't satisfied. Like the shopkeeper, at times, I felt there was no way out.

Luckily, the more I learned about OCD, the more I realised that OCD doesn't have the power of a 'real gangster'. It cannot follow through on any of its threats; neither can it back up its claims to keep you safe from anything the universe throws at you.

Chapter 21

Dealing with a compulsion to neutralise

After working as an assistant psychologist for about 18 months I was accepted onto a doctorate course in Clinical Psychology and I was now a trainee clinical psychologist. In order to fight the bully I had to find a way to reduce my neutralising behaviours. This meant noticing many of the things that I did to reduce or neutralise my emotional distress, such as ordering and repeating behaviours, and then finding a way to prevent myself carrying out these unnecessary behaviours. The most effective method that I'd heard could delay, and eventually prevent the carrying out of neutralising behaviours, was accepting feelings. I worked hard on accepting feelings and it took me a good couple of years to learn how to master the approach.

I mentioned earlier that many OCD sufferers tend to react to their intrusive thoughts by carrying out behaviours designed to either make their thoughts feel less real, or to remove their emotion. For most OCD sufferers their strategies are very individualised. They may do things repetitively; check things; complete behaviours in a certain order; go through particular thinking processes in their minds; keep hold of things; and/or carry out rituals. The ways that people neutralise or behave towards intrusive thoughts are numerous.

Through my personal experience with OCD I learnt to rate my feeling of a need to respond, which I categorised on three levels: level one was an itch; level two was an urge; and level three was a compulsion. Over time I learnt how to deal with each of them.

Level one – An itch

Most people probably think, 'What's the harm in scratching an itch?' After all, it's natural to scratch and it gives temporary relief. I defined scratching an OCD itch as a neutralising behaviour that I carried out as a result of habit, rather than in connection to an intrusive thought. For example, 'I might as well just check the locks once more, it won't do any harm!' You might think 'Is that really a problem?' But I recognised that scratching an OCD itch tended to make me feel more anxious later, and it could develop into an urge.

Level two – An urge

I noticed that the urge level to neutralise was difficult to resist, and it was much stronger than an itch. An urge would come in a wave that felt as if it was going to get higher and higher until it overwhelmed me. So, to take my previous example, if my need to check door locks was at an urge level the thought of checking door locks would come back at regular intervals, each time with higher levels of uncomfortable feeling. I noticed that if I waited long enough the uncomfortable feeling would eventually reach the highest level it could; following this it would subside. I learnt that if I surfed the urge, the neutralising behaviour would become much easier to drop and somehow become less important. I also recognised through trial and error that the reverse occurred. If I carried out a neutralising behaviour or neutralising thinking pattern (for example, continually counting all of my bank balances in my head) at an urge level it could lead to a compulsion.

Level 3 – A compulsion

I noticed that the compulsion level was the highest and most difficult to resist. I felt that I had to go along with it to obtain some kind of relief. This was the hardest level to deal with and I often needed to come up with very imaginative strategies to prevent myself from carrying out a neutralising behaviour.

I've drawn a diagram above that shows roughly how things tended to progress for me. I found that resisting at a compulsive phase was the most difficult. My feelings felt static, as if they were never going to change. It felt very uncomfortable, but I recognised that if I stayed with my uncomfortable feelings for long enough without

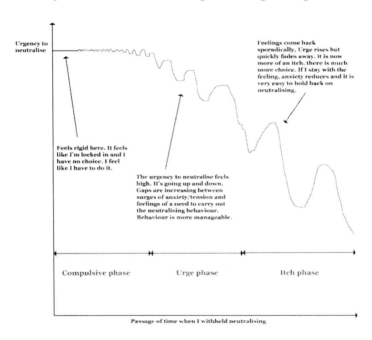

Urgency to neutralise

Feelings come back sporadically. Urge rises but quickly fades away, it is now more of an itch, there is much more choice. If I stay with the feeling, anxiety reduces and it is very easy to hold back on neutralising.

Feels rigid here. It feels like I'm locked in and I have no choice. I feel like I have to do it.

The urgency to neutralise feels high. It's going up and down. Gaps are increasing between surges of anxiety/tension and feelings of a need to carry out the neutralising behaviour. Behaviour is more manageable.

Compulsive phase   Urge phase   Itch phase

Passage of time when I withheld neutralising

neutralising they would begin to shake, wobble or shimmer just slightly. Following that, I noticed waves of urgency going up and down, but with a general downward trend. The longer I stayed without neutralising, the easier it was to go with the waves. The waves gradually grew further apart and the intensity reduced until the feeling passed.

I thought back to the 'I'm going to get you!' kid who I classed as the worst kind of bully and thought, 'What would I do with the knowledge that I have now? What would happen if I wasn't so frightened of this bully?'

Of course the answer was clear. I would continue travelling the same route home; I wouldn't change my clothes; I would carry on completely as normal. If I bumped into the bully I would ask him to do his worst and deal with him head on at the time.

Over time I learnt to do exactly the same thing with my intrusive thoughts.

Chapter 22
Noticing the neutralisers

I found that a key part of learning how to combat OCD was recognising what I was dealing with. I came to realise that OCD had many faces. Generally, as soon as I spotted one of its many faces it would change into something else. I used to think of it as a master of disguise, not unlike the character Moriarty in the *Sherlock Holmes* stories.

I found that my OCD neutralisers needed to be trimmed on a regular basis to stop them getting out of hand. I viewed my trimming process as like looking after a garden; just as with a garden, it is important to look for weeds and pull them up to stop them taking hold. I took the same attitude to my OCD, and from time to time used a compulsions rating scale to see if I needed to do any trimming back or weeding. I have placed a copy of one of my questionnaires on the next page. The scoring for this questionnaire is in the appendix of this book for those who are interested.

In my experience, behavioural compulsions were generally the simplest to drop because they were the easiest to spot. Pure compulsions, which are mental processes that you carry out repetitively in your mind, were the most difficult to drop. My pure compulsions had become quite sophisticated and difficult to notice. I usually felt drained when I was carrying them out.

Table 1. Compulsion questionnaire

Please mark how much you have been affected by the following compulsions
(where 0 = not at all, 1 = some, 2 = a lot, and 3 = severely)

#					
1	Arranging things in the environment or in the mind in a certain order.	(0)	(1)	(2)	(3)
2	Buying things that are not really needed for fear of running out.	(0)	(1)	(2)	(3)
3	Deliberately thinking of ways to avoid situations where perceived physical defect/s may be more noticeable.	(0)	(1)	(2)	(3)
4	Seeking reassurance as a result of having bad thoughts about others.	(0)	(1)	(2)	(3)
5	Saving or collecting items that don't really need to be saved.	(0)	(1)	(2)	(3)
6	Mentally repetitively inspecting scenarios where perceived illness could have been contracted, for example, sexually transmitted diseases, such as AIDS, hepatitis, etc.	(0)	(1)	(2)	(3)
7	Keeping items as they may one day become useful.	(0)	(1)	(2)	(3)
8	Over washing hands, or body through bathing or showering. Needing to wash in a particular way.	(0)	(1)	(2)	(3)
9	Mental rehearsal of the same cognitions over and over again, or saying the same things over and over again like a mantra.	(0)	(1)	(2)	(3)
10	Photographing perceived defect/s, looking in the mirror using many different angles to inspect perceived defect/s.	(0)	(1)	(2)	(3)
11	Continuously checking the self or loved ones with medical devices, e.g., blood pressure machine, thermometer etc.	(0)	(1)	(2)	(3)
12	Checking and rechecking the same Internet pages to make sure that nothing has changed, for example Facebook, or continuously listening to the news to make sure that nothing has happened to loved ones.	(0)	(1)	(2)	(3)
13	Checking journeys you have taken, retracing steps, going back to somewhere you have already been to check that everything is in order.	(0)	(1)	(2)	(3)
14	Acts of self-harm such as picking skin or self-mutilation to counteract bad thoughts.	(0)	(1)	(2)	(3)
15	Overuse of particular sprays or disinfectants.	(0)	(1)	(2)	(3)
16	Checking that physical things are in order, for example, doors, cars, appliances, jars, plugs, wallets, purses, bags, mobile phones, lockers to make sure things are as they should be.	(0)	(1)	(2)	(3)
17	Avoiding coming into contact with people, places or particular items that are viewed as contaminated, or throwing away things that have been contaminated.	(0)	(1)	(2)	(3)
18	Checking body for particular perceived defect/s.	(0)	(1)	(2)	(3)
19	Completing specific activities a specific number of times, touching safe objects, superstitious behaviour that takes up a lot of time.	(0)	(1)	(2)	(3)
20	Behaviours designed to counteract bad thoughts.	(0)	(1)	(2)	(3)
21	Spending large amounts of time on the Internet researching disease connected to the self or loved ones.	(0)	(1)	(2)	(3)

Table 1. Compulsion questionnaire (Continued)

Please mark how much you have been affected by the following compulsions
(where 0 = not at all, 1 = some, 2 = a lot, and 3 = severely)

22	Need to confess to somebody about thoughts.	⓪	①	②	③
23	Continuously phoning or texting relatives or loved ones to check that they are OK.	⓪	①	②	③
24	Wearing gloves to avoid contamination.	⓪	①	②	③
25	Writing and rewriting things.	⓪	①	②	③
26	Checking doors, locks and windows to make sure they are locked.	⓪	①	②	③
27	Over cleaning household items or objects.	⓪	①	②	③
28	Continuously requesting reassurance about the health of the self or loved ones from others.	⓪	①	②	③
29	Altering appearance, adjusting appearance to hide perceived defect/s.	⓪	①	②	③
30	Keeping paperwork just in case it contains something that may be missed or important.	⓪	①	②	③
31	Counting and recounting items, for example, money or other objects.	⓪	①	②	③
32	Over cleaning particular areas of the house.	⓪	①	②	③
33	Reading and rereading things to make sure that they have been understood correctly.	⓪	①	②	③
34	Requesting repeated medical tests for the self or loved ones.	⓪	①	②	③
35	Picking up useless items from the ground.	⓪	①	②	③
36	Excessive use of makeup to hide perceived defect/s.	⓪	①	②	③
37	Continuous checking of emails, texts or other communication devices to make sure that you have not missed anything.	⓪	①	②	③
38	Requesting repeated reassurance about appearance of perceived defect/s from others.	⓪	①	②	③
39	Continuously checking the self or loved ones for pulse, heart rate, checking heart rate for an irregular beat.	⓪	①	②	③
40	Continuously refreshing memories to ensure that they are intact.	⓪	①	②	③
41	Completing mental rituals to counteract bad thoughts.	⓪	①	②	③
42	Praying for forgiveness after having bad thoughts about others.	⓪	①	②	③

Chapter 23

The architecture was still wrong

In an ideal world, it would be nice to think that you could have psychotherapy, deal with your underlying issues, and that this would fix your problems. You could then walk away from therapy and have a 'normal' life. I soon discovered that therapy wasn't going to be a magic cure-all. It just didn't work that way. Therapy helped me to understand much more about OCD but I still had some neurological difficulties.

Poor connections between my cingulate gyrus and other areas of my brain meant that I could still get stuck on things, and problems with my caudate nucleus connections meant that thoughts that weren't accurate would continue popping into my awareness. The main advantage that I had now compared to before was that I knew what was going on.

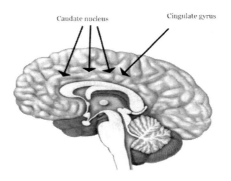

Caudate nucleus

Cingulate gyrus

I discovered that there were three main brain structures that I needed to know much more about to react differently in my life. These brain areas were the neo-cortex, the pre-frontal cortex, and the sub-cortical region – which contains the amygdala and the limbic system. I will describe these areas below.

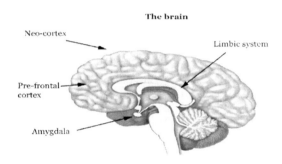

The neo-cortex and pre-frontal cortex

I learnt that the neo-cortex was the part of the brain responsible for thinking, planning, and logical thought. However, the most interesting part of the brain that I thought might help me with my OCD was the pre-frontal cortex, which I discovered was essential for psychological wellness. If you haven't heard of the pre-frontal cortex, it sits on top of the limbic system and acts as a communication system between the neo-cortex and the sub-cortical region. It has many important functions. It quietens down noise in the mind and it can call off emotional reactions created by sub-cortical regions. This part of the brain helps us to think about our thinking and helps us to weigh up choices.

The brain

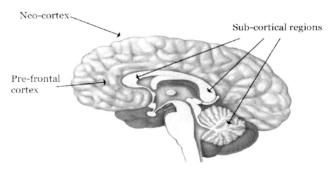

The sub-cortical regions

Relevant to my early experiences of OCD I discovered that sub-cortical regions of the brain became highly active when we experience perceived threat; whether real or imagined. If you haven't heard of the sub-cortical region, it takes its name because it is located underneath the brain's outer cortex area. Many people describe it as the primitive or animal brain, as we share similar brain structures with all mammals. The amygdala, which is located on both sides of the brain in the sub-cortical region, is responsible for activating emotions such as anxiety.

I figured that as a child I must have been highly anxious most of the time and because of this my sub-cortical region had been firing off a lot. I read research that suggested that when people become highly anxious sub-cortical brain regions release neurochemicals known as **catecholamines**, which improve the way in which primitive brain regions function. In lay terms, catecholamines work a bit like a turbo-boost or a power-up for the animal brain. When primitive brain regions become more active, people become aware of all of their senses. As a result of this, they may see, hear, feel, taste and smell things more. This process is not without problems, however. Catecholamines, although enhancing the effects of the sub-cortical region, leach or spread into the nearby pre-frontal cortex and stop it functioning effectively. This leaching effect is usually only temporary. When the threat dies down and neurochemicals are reabsorbed, the pre-frontal cortex starts to work normally as before. Things started to click into place for me when I heard how this system worked. 'That's why your mind goes blank when you're anxious!' I thought to myself. This also explains to me why people often got hijacked by their emotions. With the pre-frontal cortex and neo-cortex cut off, the animal is left to take care of things, sometimes with unfortunate results.

I also read that if we experience threat over long periods of time, the continuous release of catecholamines by sub-cortical regions can gradually wear away – or cause atrophy to – the pre-frontal cortex located right next to it. I discovered that this generally results in the pre-frontal cortex operating much less effectively.

I learnt that when the pre-frontal cortex goes off-line or begins to work less effectively, we lose our ability to calm ourselves and we can start to feel more agitated about things that we weren't really bothered about before. This occurs as the pre-frontal cortex can no longer supress emotional reactions triggered by sub-cortical regions. The neo-cortex (thinking/analytical brain), which lies just above it, is also unable to function effectively as it relies heavily on the pre-frontal cortex to make decisions and direct attentional resources.

So now I understood exactly what was happening to me. But it still didn't really change any of the problems that I had with my brain! I still needed to do something differently, but what could it be? I decided to practise exercises that I'd heard might strengthen my pre-frontal cortex, such as mindfulness and working memory training, and I put a lot of attention into learning how to manage my emotions. When I had frightening thoughts I practised staying with my feelings, which led to my feelings becoming much less intense and bearable. This in turn made the thoughts I experienced feel much less real. I've put a copy of the emotions exercise that I use in the appendix of this book if you're interested.

I also dropped safety behaviours as I recognised that carrying out safety behaviours tended to keep fear in place. By safety behaviours, I mean the kinds of behaviours that I used to cope with my anxiety: like holding my breath or distracting myself. Most of us use safety behaviours, not only because our natural inclination is to avoid high levels of fear, but also because they help us to avoid concerns and fears about potential negative outcomes. However, a major problem with using avoidance and safety behaviours where anxiety is concerned is that the more we carry out safety behaviours the more engrained safety behaviours and avoidance strategies become. I learnt as a psychology undergraduate that we are preprogramed to experience a sense of relief when we carry out a behaviour that removes pain or reduces worry. In psychological terms this process is referred to as negative reinforcement — By engaging in a certain behaviour we can remove the pain associated with feared negative consequences. Over time as processes are repeated and memory pathways are laid down we begin to carry out these behaviours automatically without thinking. Ultimately, the more that we use avoidant strategies and safety behaviours the less anxiety we experience. In this respect, we feel as though we are dealing successfully with the problem. However, as time progresses more situations that trigger anxiety are likely to occur, leading to more withdrawal. This can lead to a loss of confidence accompanied by a feeling of restriction, which further reduces confidence.

I'm an animal

Although I knew logically that I must be sharing a shell with an animal, because I did the same things that all animals do, it hadn't really clicked in my mind that I needed the animal part to co-operate to make anything happen. Luckily, the right-hand side of my brain sent me an image of a horse and rider. This symbolic image of a person riding a horse made complete sense to me. The neo-cortex was the rider and decided where the horse might go; the primitive mind was the horse and took the rider where it needed to go. The rider part of me needed to learn how to look after the animal and to take the animal's needs into account in order to get the best out of it.

To fully understand this, I needed to recognise that the animal was in charge of emotions, but needed help to regulate them. As I observed myself I noticed that the animal mind tended to produce an emotional response to anything that might concern it at a primitive level, such as food, health, shelter, safety, procreation, and especially social status. It seemed unconcerned about most other things.

I also noticed that the animal mind had quite a strong reaction to intrusive thoughts. 'That's why thoughts affect the way that we feel,' I thought to myself. 'If I

113

carry out any safety behaviour or neutralising behaviour in response to intrusive thoughts I will be telling the animal mind that the threat was valid in some kind of way. This will make my animal's anxiety levels higher and I will live in fear.'

Chapter 24

Dealing with the aftermath

As I began to put into practice what I had learnt, I became much better at reacting to intrusive thoughts. I knew exactly what they were. I also recognised where they might focus. They focused mainly on my health, as this was still an area of vulnerability, but they would diverge into other areas as well. Like the time I was at our local supermarket and the cashier had her till open, revealing a large wad of cash. I had a vivid image of putting my hand in the till, grabbing the cash, and running off with it. I didn't need the money as I had plenty available in my bank account at the time.

There was also the occasion when I was driving and I was a little tired. I had an intrusive thought that told me that although I thought I was driving, I was really dreaming that I was driving, and that in fact I was asleep at the wheel. Then there was the time when I was looking after my daughter Christabelle. Christabelle was a baby and she was crying and moaning. Nothing I was doing seemed to help. I was holding her in my arms when suddenly I had a vivid intrusive thought of throwing her against a wall. I smiled to myself and thought, 'That's interesting' and carried on looking after Christablle.

This thought helped me to recognise what it was like for many people who have intrusive thoughts about harming their baby and, like me, would never act on it. A lot of mothers I've worked with told me that they didn't know what to do with their intrusive thoughts and eventually went to their GP or a health professional thinking that they were dangerous in some way. In therapy they told me that they feared social services would be called and that their child or children would be taken away. They were petrified about approaching their doctor. Any doctor who has read the research on OCD will recognise that the risk of OCD sufferers acting on their intrusive thoughts is next to zero. However, unfortunately, every so often there is a doctor who doesn't quite know what he or she is doing who calls social services. This generally makes the situation ten times worse. Social services generally call back saying that they are not concerned, and tell the doctor to refer their patient to a mental health expert.

Chapter 25

Is it a compulsion or is it a habit?

As time progressed, I learnt how to practise managing my emotions, observe my thoughts, reduce my safety behaviours, and live healthily. My life had improved a lot, but I recognised that I still had a lot of unhelpful habits. I noticed that I still carried out repetitive behaviours when there was no need to, even when I didn't have any intrusive thoughts or distressing emotions. I guessed these repetitive behaviours must have come about as a result of habit.

I read that a lot of repetitive and habitual behaviour was hardwired into a sub-cortical part of the brain called the basal ganglia. This hardwiring helps the brain to work more efficiently. To change the use of unhelpful habits, I would need to catch myself while I was using unhelpful habits, and then break the pattern. I recognised that I had collected an enormous number of habits after having OCD for years. For example, I noticed that I had a habit of adding up all of the available funds in my bank and savings accounts in my head. I did this over and over again, even though I knew how much money I had available. It was a hangover from a pure compulsion that I used to carry out. There was no longer any intrusive thought or painful emotion that accompanied this behaviour and I recognised that I was wasting valuable mental energy carrying out a pretty useless cognitive process. Carrying out these repetitive behaviours over and over again left me feeling dead inside. It was a bit like eating paper and expecting to receive some kind of nutritional value from it. I recognised that I would need to practise using new positive habits over and over again. I found that if I completed new behaviours enough times they would eventually click into place automatically, just as the old ones did before. I realised that this process would take time, however, as brain wiring in the basal ganglia wouldn't grow instantaneously.

I'll give you just one example of a habit that I changed, otherwise this book would be full of them. I noticed that I carried out a routine when using public restrooms. I would normally use my foot to open a restroom door, and then wash my hands straight away. I would have a quick look around to see if anyone noticed what I was doing. I would then use a tissue to open and close restroom doors, and use the same tissue to flush the lavatory before I used it. I would never sit on a lavatory seat, unless I had carefully placed layers of bath tissue – toilet paper to English people – over it. After I had finished using the lavatory I would use another tissue to flush the lavatory, and the same tissue to open the cubicle door. I would then throw the tissue in the water as the lavatory was flushing, while I was on my way out. I would then use the back of my hands or my elbows to turn taps on and off to wash my hands once more. It was quite an elaborate routine. I did it so automatically that I didn't even realise what I was doing. I decided to dispense with most of this, and instead just refrained from touching doors on the way out of the restroom after washing my hands properly.

Chapter 26
Difficulty with transitions

As I continued my training in Psychology I began to recognise that my OCD tended to flare up during times of major transition. I rationalised to myself that transitions were times of increased uncertainty for me as I needed to cope with the unknown. Generally, I would become more obsessive during these periods. As I mentioned previously, obsessive behaviour can sometimes create an illusion of external order that helps to compensate for internal chaos. I think that this happens to a lot of people who have had OCD.

My poor partner Nicola had to put up with my obsessive behaviour for years. When I was stuck in one of my obsessions, Nicola found it difficult to gain my attention, as I found it incredibly hard to detach from whatever I was fixated on. I'm sure that Nicola realised that my behaviour wasn't personal, but it was frustrating for her nevertheless. Sometimes when Nicola prepared a meal and it was time to eat, separating myself from whatever I was obsessing over felt extremely difficult. Whatever I was fixated on felt like the most important thing in the world. More important than food, more important than the time and effort that Nicola had put into preparing a meal, and more important than Nicola's feelings. Each time I managed to detach from an obsession I wondered why on earth it was so important.

Once I was able to detach from an obsession I could almost resemble a normal human being. I recognised that if I spent too much time obsessing over anything it would continue running in the background of my mind, even when I was doing other things like having conversations or going for a walk. I was like Gollum in J.R.R. Tolkien's trilogy *The Lord of the Rings*, obsessed with 'my precious', the 'ruling ring'.

Brain training

With my cognitive difficulties in mind I thought that it might be beneficial to do brain training as I'd heard that this could improve things. 'What's the harm?' I thought; 'after all, my brain does need training.' I downloaded a brain training application onto my phone.

Once I began playing brain-training games, I found them very difficult to leave alone. I kept looking up my scores and comparing them with scores from other people throughout the world. Like anything else I became fixated on, I really didn't like being interrupted when I was playing these games. My focus was on trying to get into the top ten in the world in various parts of the game, which I achieved for short-lived periods. One day I noticed there was an area where you could check your usage of the game. I was shocked when I saw the results. I was one of the top users of the game in the world, in terms of hours played on the game. Users included teenagers without jobs, and I had a full-time job, two children, and a partner.

My fixation or addiction had crept up on me without me realising it. Like so many things that I'd become obsessive about before, I didn't have insight into the fact that I had got caught up in it. I decided to delete the brain-training app from my phone. I brought it back onto my phone on a few occasions due to boredom. But each time I did that I recognised that it had started to become an obsession once more, and I needed to delete it again. I knew it had become a problem when I started to get angry when my daughter Christabelle interrupted me when I was playing it.

The running man

You might think that running could be viewed as a healthy activity and relatively harmless, but anything can be difficult if you are obsessive.

I started off running for fun at a running club called St Edmunds Pacers. I joined the club just to take part in their track training nights and to accompany my daughter Christabelle. Christabelle was shy as a youngster and she didn't like going to new activities on her own, so my son Harvey and I joined the running club as well. We were all put into different age groups for training. Joining the running club appeared to be a great idea at the time, because it was something that my children and I could do at the same place and same time, although not together.

Track work involved running for a short period at quite a fast pace, and then stopping for a brief interval to get your breath back. The runners called this interval or fartlek training. As an adult I have always had a large muscular frame, big bones, and I'm 6ft 2in (1.88m). When I joined the running club I was a bit overweight and weighed in at about 230lb (105kg). As you might imagine, I didn't have the best body type for joining a cross-country running club. I would have been better suited to being either a forward in a rugby team or a defender in an American football team. Nevertheless, I thought at the time it was a good idea to join the running club.

One day I brought a friend with me who was similar in size to me. We were just being lapped for the third or fourth time by one of the better runners, Pete Golding, when he stopped for a brief chat with us. 'It's great to see you big guys here running at the club', he said. 'People out there…' he continued, pointing at something that seemed a long way off in the distance, 'will see you guys on the track and think to themselves, "look at those big guys down there running on the track. If they can do it, I can do it!"' As Peter was running off, a thought got stuck in my mind: 'I'm a big guy! I look big, even from a distance!' My mind immediately translated Peter's words into 'I'm fat'. To be honest, I hadn't really thought that I was fat before. But, compared to the average male runner at the club with a height of about 5ft 9in, and weighing in at 140–150lb (63–68kg) which was Peter's build, I must have seemed like a giant.

Peter hadn't meant to be disparaging in any way; he was one of the friendliest and most supportive people you could possibly meet. I thought to myself, 'Perhaps I could move up to training twice a week? What would be the harm in it?' A little while later I was going down to the track twice a week, and eventually got to know a lot of the other runners. The runners were a friendly, sociable group. Many of them asked me if I had ever thought about doing a race series called the 'Friday 5s'. As you might guess, it was a five-mile race that was run five times a year on a Friday evening. 'No!' I said, 'I'm not getting involved with anything like that. I'm just here to get a bit fitter.'

Other runners continued to ask me about doing races, perhaps as a way of making conversation. After a while I relented and decided to enter a race. When I got to my first race, which was held at a park in Bury St Edmunds,

Suffolk, there were already hundreds of people there. Runners from lots of different clubs from the region were dressed in their club regalia. It was a hive of activity. Many runners seemed to think that the race was very important. They were doing warm-ups, dynamic stretches, and little sprints. They were doing the kinds of exercises that I'd seen professional athletes do on the TV. I laughed with Nicola, who had come along to support me, at how seriously some of these runners were taking the race.

I ran the five-mile cross-country race in just over 38 minutes. I was pretty pleased with myself for finishing about halfway in the whole group of people. I'd run the race without wearing a club shirt, so the following Monday, the secretary of the running club presented me with a St Edmunds Pacers runner's vest. I felt honoured to be given the vest, but what I didn't quite realise at the time was that it activated my sense of responsibility. I thought to myself, 'I've been given a vest! The club needs me!' That was when my problem with running started.

After about six months I had become completely obsessed with running. I had built up my running mileage to about 60 miles (96km) a week or more. Sometimes, I was running twice per day and it was taking up huge amounts of my time. I lost over 50lb (23kg) in weight. I completely changed my diet, and I was eating six meals a day. Even though I was about 42 or 43 by this time, in my obsessive mindset I imagined that I was a professional athlete, and work was very much my secondary occupation. I researched what professional athletes did and I did the same things: ice baths; a restricted diet; wholegrain foods; no refined sugar; sports massages; strength training; hill training and mountain running. I employed my own yoga instructor. I read dozens of books on running. I bought the best shoes and anything that might give me a slight edge or knock a second or two off my time. I bought a heart-rate monitor to ensure that I could run at 90% of my maximum heart rate in every race. My maximum heart rate was quite high at about 190 beats per minute, so I found that I needed to race at a constant 172 beats per minute. This meant that I was in pain in each race.

Within a year I was doing exactly the same thing as the runners I'd laughed about the year before. I was the same as them, doing dynamic stretches, short sprints, and warm-ups. I wore compression clothing, and drank beetroot juice three hours before a race, even though it tasted disgusting, and made me feel ill. I had become a very fast cross-country runner. I could run at a six-minute-mile pace for long periods. This was quite fast for someone who had big bones and a 6ft 2in frame. Even though I wasn't cut out physically to be a long-distance runner, I didn't care. All my focus was on races. I started to think to myself, 'If I could just lose a bit more weight, I could decrease my running times still further.' My partner Nicola said that she didn't find the skinny look I had attractive, as in her mind I had begun to look smaller than her. But I thought to myself, 'Appearance doesn't matter. How shallow it is to think that way!'

Within two years I had become the fastest runner in my age group at the running club and I had won my first trophy. I had done well at running not due to any particular talent or ability, but because I took it to extreme levels. I trained more than anyone else. All I could think about was running. I was fixated and obsessed. I was looking up my running data on websites such as the 'Power of 10' and 'UK Athletics'. I looked up other runners as well. I asked myself, what would I need to do to match their times? People who hadn't seen me for a while noticed my dramatic weight loss and thought I was seriously ill, as I'd lost more than a fifth of my body mass in a short period of time. I had lost a lot of muscle tissue as well as fat.

After a while I suddenly realised what had been happening. How could I have had such a lack of personal insight? I had let my obsessive behaviour creep up and take me over.

I tried to wean myself off running by having stern talks with myself. My conversation went something along the lines of, 'James, what are you doing this for? You're too old to become an Olympic athlete. You've got the wrong body shape for cross-country running. You have nothing to prove! You're probably going to damage your body if you keep this up long term.' However, I still found it very difficult to detach from my obsession, as I had friends at the running club and there was a social element attached to it.

Then, perhaps luckily, I had a slight muscle injury that stopped me running for a week or two, and I began to fully recognise what I was doing. I decided that I would take a break from running before things deteriorated even further. I discontinued running competitively, but carried on running recreationally. The funny thing was, just like my previous obsessions, I could walk away from competitive running just like that and not look back. But I didn't realise at the time that was true only as long as I had something else to fixate on instead.

Chapter 28

If you can't beat it, join it

As I looked back on my obsessive behaviour, I realised that it was very unlikely that I would ever be able to change significantly. Being obsessive was so hardwired into my brain and so entrenched in my personality that, realistically, it was going to be a challenge to be different. If I am really honest, I also recognised that being obsessive offered me so much that I didn't really want to change.

But then I received a psychological challenge from my daughter Christabelle. Since she had learnt to speak, her mother Nicola and I noticed that she had very highly developed psychological knowledge. We were amazed at her uncanny ability to see straight through people. I initially put her ability down to having two parents as psychologists. More latterly, I've thought that sometimes people are simply born gifted in certain areas, and Christabelle seemed to be born with very high levels of emotional intelligence. When I asked her about the motivations of her friends, she could see straight through their defences to their psychological vulnerability. She could interpret my adult friends very accurately as well, and could give psychological explanations for their behaviour. I have to admit that she has more ability than me, and I'm a trained psychologist. Sometimes if I had problems with friends that I was stuck with, I would ask Christabelle and she would explain what they were thinking to me.

One day I was reading one of Christabelle's English essays. She was still a child but she could describe very complex psychological concepts. She wrote about the experience of a girl and her relationship with her father. She wrote, 'He was there, but he wasn't there. He'd left his outer presence behind, but he'd gone somewhere else, and she missed him.' This was heart-wrenching to read. I felt extremely guilty as I immediately realised that she was describing me.

I had completed the majority of Christabelle's childcare when she was a small child, but when she got a bit older I got side-tracked by obsessive behaviours as I struggled to deal with significant challenges that I felt existed in the adult world. As was my pattern back then, my tendency to become obsessive was an attempt to create a semblance of order to compensate for my sense of inner turmoil. This must have been very difficult for Christabelle to adjust to. I recognised that if I became overly fixated on anything it caused a reduction in the quality of my relationships. It left people close to me, like Nicola, my children, friends and family, looking on from the outside, perhaps wondering when I was going to come back to them. I also noticed that Nicola, my family, my friends, and my children loved it when I returned to them at an emotional level, even though I had been present physically all along.

After reading Christabelle's essay I knew that I couldn't pretend that my tendency to being obsessive didn't affect others, and I knew that my obsessive behaviour could fixate on any area of my life. For example, on one occasion I became aware that it was creeping into a football team that I was managing. I had just attended an English Football Association training course and I had begun to think about how I could improve the team

I was managing. I thought to myself, 'Maybe I could put on extra training sessions, teach the players how to complete complex drills, increase the endurance of the players.' But then I caught myself. 'Hold on a minute! Steady on! I think that you're forgetting that these children are only 11 years old! This is your son's football team. These boys are playing football for fun and to be with their friends. They're not trying to be professional football players. If they were going to be professionals they'd have been picked up by the big teams already. It doesn't really matter what happens as long as they enjoy themselves.' But, seriously, these were the types of thought patterns that I deal with all the time.

The words of the novelist Sir Kingsley Amis came to mind. Amis wrote of his romping libido: 'It was like being chained to an idiot for 50 years.' I could identify with this. For me, though, I'd spent nearly 50 years of my life being chained to a savant. I found that just as difficult!

Chapter 29
The introduction of Frederik

Although my tendency to be obsessive over the years gave me some problems, I wanted to think warmly towards that part of myself because it helped me achieve a lot as well. While researching information for my doctorate in clinical psychology I read about the work of Hazel Markus and Paula Nurius. They were very influential in the field of psychology due to their theory of 'possible selves'. They suggested that we all had different self-concepts inhabiting our persona, and that different self-concepts could come on-line depending on the context in which we operate. Markus and Nurius said that our problem-solving ability could differ according to the self-concept that was on-line at any one point in time. Their idea is not to be confused with Dissociative Identity Disorder (DID), where it is suggested that each self-concept has no awareness of the existence of other self-concepts. In a healthy, functioning human, self-concepts will all be aware of one another and will come on-line when required. It's a bit like your personality is a minibus carrying several passengers. Depending on where the bus is being driven, different passengers will take over the driving. The passengers normally get along very well and co-operate with each other.

Markus and Nurius's argument was that the person we are in any given situation may be very different depending on the people we come into contact with. In short, we change according to who we're with. All of our potential selves will not be on-line at the same time. For example, we could have a professional self; a self with close friends; a self with a partner; a self with our parents; and a self with our children. The number of potential selves that anyone has depends on how many relationships they have. Possible selves theory made sense to me because I noticed that I could be a very different person at work compared to the person I was with friends. It seemed that my psychologist-self was very highly developed in comparison to the self I was around friends. I noticed that I was a different person with each of my children.

I had learned through my study of psychology that naming and externalising an aspect of the self can reduce the power that it exerts over you. Using a combination of externalising and possible selves theory I decided to give my obsessive self-concept a name. I called him Frederik.

In order to externalise Frederik properly, I needed to create an image of what he looked like. Thinking about his characteristics, I imagined Frederik as highly self-negligent, intelligent, and possibly on the autistic spectrum. I visualised him as looking like me, but with long greasy hair and wearing inappropriate clothes, as appearance was irrelevant to him. He had thick spectacles with multiple lenses that looked more like binoculars than glasses. He was extremely short-sighted and he could never see the big picture, so had a tendency to focus on fine details or minutiae using his binocular glasses. Frederik was very good at looking at the fine print in documents. He could work for many hours without a break. He didn't wash or brush his teeth, as in his mind this took up too much valuable time. Eating was inconvenient, so if he couldn't bypass eating altogether he would eat as quickly as possible to get it out of the way. He didn't want to spend time with friends because that wasted time that he could be spending on his obsession. Frederik hated having his work interrupted. Whatever he was doing at any particular time was the most important thing in the world to him. Frederik could work on his obsession while bombs were going off around him. He was that focused! Frederik was like a train on a railway track. Once he got rolling he could build up huge speed and momentum, but he was also incredibly difficult to stop. Frederik also had a one-track mind. He had tunnel vision and wasn't able to change direction once he had set his mind on something. He didn't know how to take shortcuts, or how to slow down. As a result, he would often go well past his stop.

I recognised that I really needed to build a better relationship with Frederik, because he didn't like being left out. I also didn't want him continually taking the wheel of my minibus just because he thought he was the best driver. I was aware that when I had tried to shut him out in the past he had a tendency to disguise himself, creep up on me and gradually take over my hobbies and interests without me noticing. Of course, Frederik thought he could do a much better job on my hobbies than other parts of me. If Frederik got involved with anything it would then become the most important thing in the world.

I considered the benefits of having Frederik. Would I have achieved a career in Clinical Psychology without him? Possibly, but Frederik did help me by getting fixated on achieving a first-class degree. It would have been much more difficult to obtain interviews as an assistant psychologist without a good degree. A clinical psychologist also knows that if he or she employs an assistant with a first-class degree, they are likely to be employing someone who is quite obsessive. Obsessive assistants often have excellent report writing skills, and carry out first-rate clinical work.

How could I help Frederik to co-operate better alongside my other self-concepts? I recognised that Frederik thought that he could help me in everything, which included running, football management, relationships, sleep, food, hobbies, physical and mental health. But he probably overestimated his abilities to deal with many areas of my life; I needed to find a way to hold him back and focus him on projects where he might be more useful. Metaphorically speaking, I needed to view Frederik like a disruptive child. I needed to keep Frederik close, at the forefront of my mind, where I could keep an eye on him. I didn't want him pulling strings in the background or drifting into my unconscious and reinventing himself. Based on the amount of psychological knowledge he had access to, it could be very difficult to reign him in if I cut him loose. I also didn't want him gradually creeping into things like the management of my son's football team, as he did on one occasion. To Frederik, the idea that the kids were 10 or 11 years old was irrelevant. He would expect children to have the mentality of professional athletes. Managing a children's football team is the last place where I would want Frederik to get involved. If I could keep him focused on a safe obsession that could create some value, then hopefully there wouldn't be enough room for him to work on other things at the same time.

I also knew that I needed to limit the amount of time Frederik spent fixating on things. On occasions I gave him free reign on work projects because I needed him.

But I found if I gave Frederik too much time on any obsession it would leave me feeling drained of energy. I would then start to feel switched off emotionally to things around me. Frederik would also be there in the back of my mind thinking of his latest ideas, while I was trying to do activities like yoga or mindfulness.

I set aside time for Frederik to complete difficult work projects, like writing policies and procedures, creating websites, designing work-based leaflets and literature, resolving complex legal problems, creating professional worksheets, designing book covers, editing books, reviewing material, and improving therapeutic interventions. On each occasion I needed to ask myself: is Frederik going to add some benefit if I ask him to obsess over this?

I recognised that what I also needed to do was to learn how to redirect Frederik. If I noticed that Frederik was trying to encroach on any areas of my life that I considered weren't safe, I would mentally redirect him to the project that I had given him. I also needed to learn how to disengage him when he was fixated on something, as he found it very difficult to stop. He wasn't happy about being interrupted from what he was fixated on by having to go to work, to do household chores, or eat meals. I would imagine myself saying to Frederik, 'It's OK to be flexible. It's OK to stop now. You can come back to it later.'

I found that the more I externalised Frederik and gave him something productive to focus on, the easier he became to manage. To an outsider I realise that what I'm saying sounds quite insane! But I also figure that as I have insight into what I'm talking about, this doesn't count as insanity.

I noticed that Frederik worked better if I separated him from my other self-concepts. He was best working alone. Frederik liked structure and he needed to be kept busy, so I made sure that he always had something that he could obsess over. I also knew that if I had a difficult problem that needed to be solved I could count on him. He was incredibly dependable, and would keep on going and going until the job was done, no matter how difficult the material. Frederik just didn't know how to give up on something. I would need other parts of myself to pull the plug on projects if they weren't working.

I found Frederik proved essential in completing tasks that other parts of my self had no interest in. In situations where colleagues had legal difficulties, he worked like a lawyer, leaving no stone unturned. He would have legal minutiae covered to such an extent that anyone challenging his arguments would find it very difficult to disagree with him. In these areas he was very useful and I was happy that I could call upon him.

At the moment, I am grateful that Frederik is a part of me. I have introduced him to my family, and told them what tasks I have set him, but I haven't quite got to the stage of setting an extra place for him at the table.

Chapter 30

Conclusion

Like many people with OCD, the biggest problem that I faced as a child and a teenager was living with undiagnosed OCD. Because of this, I didn't recognise what I was dealing with. I wasn't able to connect all of the problems that I had over the years and to see that they were all part of the same thing. It's especially difficult to recognise OCD in yourself, because in so many respects it's like a master of disguise. It has access to all of your knowledge and it is as clever as you are. This makes going into battle with it futile. The hardest person to see problems in is yourself, especially when you are so close to your difficulties. It is much easier to see problems in others.

As I look back, I can't really remember a time when I wasn't obsessive. Now that I'm older, my personality seems to have been smoothed out somewhat. It's a bit like therapy has led to a lot of the rough edges being chiselled away from my character. I have now reached a kind of self-acceptance. I still get fused to things, but now I just make sure that what I get stuck to is going to be useful in some way. I don't want to forget what happened in the past. I'm happy to revisit my memories and stroke them like I would old scars that don't hurt any more.

I am mindful that my obsessiveness has the capability to reinvent itself and to come back as something new if I don't keep it at the forefront of my mind. So I now manage my obsessive behaviour very much like I would a garden. Like a gardener, I pull up weeds or unnecessary thinking patterns or neutralisers as soon as I notice them growing. This stops them taking hold. If I can keep on top of the weeds then I can really focus on the plants that I want to flourish.

I have externalised much of my obsessive nature by creating a self-concept called Frederik. Psychologically, I recognise that when I can stand back and observe Frederik I am really engaging my pre-frontal cortex. As I have already mentioned, this is a part of the brain that helps us to think about our thinking and to manage our thoughts. I also recognise that if I let my stress levels increase too much, then my pre-frontal cortex will not function so well, and it will be much more difficult to manage Frederik. If this happens, Frederik could take over, and it's better to avoid that.

To reduce my tendency to overinflate my sense of responsibility for things I often use a CBT technique called a responsibility pie. The last time I used it was to help me with my son's football team – which, incidentally, I still manage. When the team loses, some of the players don't feel too good about themselves, even though they have tried their very best, and I feel sorry for them. However, if I were to take on board too much responsibility for their feelings, Frederik would want to get involved and that wouldn't work out well.

To complete a responsibility pie I make a list of all the people who might be involved in an area of my life that I am taking responsibility for (I have placed a copy of one of my completed sheets overleaf). By the end of working on sheets like this I am able to put things in perspective. It helps me to recognise that in many areas of my life I really have very little responsibility. My job is to guide and support others, not to take charge of their lives.

Completing exercises like the responsibility pie over the years has helped me to recognise that I'm really quite a small cog in what is, in most cases, a large machine.

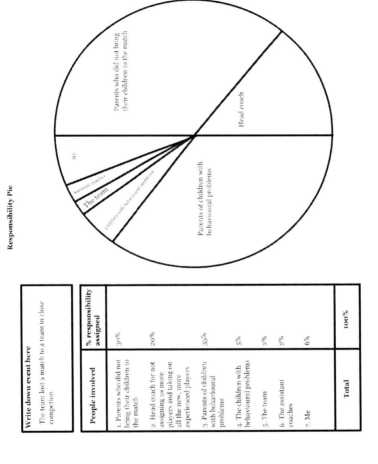

Responsibility Pie

Write down event here	
The team lost a match to a team in close competion	

People involved	% responsibility assigned
1. Parents who did not bring their children to the match	30%
2. Head coach for not assigning us more players and taking on all the new, more experienced players	20%
3. Parents of children with behavioural problems	35%
4. The children with behavioural problems	5%
5. The team	2%
6. The assistant coaches	2%
7. Me	6%
Total	**100%**

Previously, even as a small cog, I would have tried to drive the machine, and then wondered to myself why I kept breaking down.

In the past, I used alcohol quite a bit to turn my obsessiveness off, but I noticed that this caused other problems. It was a bit like throwing water onto an engine. Initially the engine would stall, but it would then burn off the water and rev up once more. The water also wasn't good for the engine. I didn't realise at the time that when the body breaks down alcohol or metabolises it, the process actually results in increased anxiety. This would ultimately result in increased obsessive behaviours and I would get caught in a vicious cycle.

I continue to use many of the exercises and coping strategies that I have learnt over the years to keep in a state of well-being. I can state categorically that if I were to stop using my coping strategies now, I would very quickly drift back into mental health problems. Complacency is a big risk factor for anyone who has experienced mental health problems.

Key points that I learnt in my journey and advice I would give others

- Recognising that I had OCD was my biggest breakthrough. Untreated OCD has the potential to create havoc.

- It is important to keep aware of any new or developing neutralisers and reduce then as quickly as possible. Leaving them without intervention is like forgetting to do your gardening for several months: you go back to it and wonder why it is so full of weeds.

- I have found that it is important to keep chipping away at OCD every day. Even small amounts of progress add up and, in general, keep problems more manageable.

- The best way to detach from a fixation is to step away from it. The more time that can be left between feeling an urge to neutralise and carrying out a neutralising behaviour, the easier the neutralising behaviour will be to drop. I found that accepting feelings makes the process feel a lot easier.

- Externalising OCD reduces its hold. I found that giving it a name also made it less powerful. My OCD started off feeling like a bully. But, after a while, just like many people who have a tendency to bully others, my OCD started to show a different side when it was understood. I have known many people who bullied others as children, but who have turned into compassionate, considerate, caring, and productive adults later.

- I learnt that the best way to harness OCD is to refuse to play its game: unless it's a game that I want to play of course!

- I found that exercises like mindfulness helped improve my ability to detach from fixations. I found that mindfulness could also reduce the power of intrusive thoughts.

Glossary

Amygdala Small area of brain tissue within the limbic system, responsible for activating the body's fight-flight-or-freeze response.

Anxiety An emotion that is experienced when the body is moving into a prepared state to deal with a potential threat.

Automatic responses Responses that occur automatically/outside of conscious awareness.

Avoidance A process of disengaging from activities.

Behavioural strategies Making an adjustment to your behaviour and monitoring the impact of resulting changes.

Catastrophic misinterpretation A frightening and exaggerated thought connected to magnification of perceived stimuli.

Catecholamines Chemical messengers used by cells to communicate with one another.

Cognitive distortions Thinking patterns that distort perceptions of reality.

Cognitive interventions Strategies based on changing mental reactions.

Cognitive models Ways of explaining how psychological distress is maintained.

Compulsive behaviour Carrying out a behaviour where no choice is involved.

Conditioned response A response that occurs automatically as a result of repeated actions towards particular stimuli.

Coping strategies Strategies that have been of some assistance in reducing distress.

Core beliefs Strongly held beliefs about the self.

Counselling psychologist A psychologist usually trained to a high level in at least three forms of therapeutic intervention.

Counter-intuitive Ideas that we would not naturally gravitate towards.

Default response An automatic response based on previous experiences and past conditioning.

Desensitising Gradually being able to tolerate a feeling by staying in a situation until it becomes more bearable.

Dissociation A mental and physical state where an individual feels a loss of connection with his or her body.

Distraction A process that individuals use to avoid experiencing painful emotions.

Experiential A process of experiencing and learning through the senses.

External focus Placing one's attention onto one's external environment.

Fixation A mental process from which you are unable to separate yourself.

Habitual behaviours Behaviours that we are inclined to do because we have done them so many times before.

Hypothesis An idea based on scientific theory.

Intrusive thoughts Thoughts that enter awareness uninvited. These thoughts are usually accompanied by heightened emotion.

Late developer A teenager who matures at a later age than is considered normal for his or her age group.

Limerence A state of mind that results from a romantic attraction to another person. It typically includes obsessive thoughts and fantasies and a desire to form or maintain a relationship with the object of love and have one's feelings reciprocated.

Mindfulness A process of staying in the present moment, bringing conscious awareness back to the present, and deliberately moving away from thoughts about the past or the future.

Mood regulation An ability to have some management of one's feelings.

Negative automatic thoughts Thoughts in the background of the mind that have the potential to keep individuals emotionally distressed.

Negative reinforcement A process of repeated behaviour in which a negative emotion is reduced, leading to a greater likelihood of the same future behaviour.

Neo-cortex Highly developed area of the mind responsible for logical, rational and analytical thinking.

Neutralise A way of eliminating distress and a behaviour that is commonly associated with repetitive physical behaviours of thinking patterns.

Phobic response An automatic response associated with heightened anxiety, connected to a specific trigger or cue.

Pre-frontal cortex An area of the brain that acts as a relay between the sub-cortical regions of the brain and the neo-cortex. It is also responsible for dampening emotional reactions and quieting the mind.

Psychotherapy The treatment of difficulties through talking therapies.

Rumination A cognitive process that involves churning of thoughts connected to the self in the past over and over in the mind.

Safety behaviours Behaviours utilised to reduce emotional distress in the short term.

Self-fulfilling prophecy When something occurs despite your very best attempts to prevent that particular thing occurring.

Self-perpetuating A situation that is kept in place through its own actions.

Sub-cortical regions Brain areas located in the lower half of the brain.

Suppressing emotions An act of pushing down painful or upsetting feelings.

Transactional analysis A form of psychotherapy that seeks to develop parental (critical and nurturing), adult (rational), and childlike (intuitive and dependent) parts of the personality.

Traumatic incidents Events that have occurred in the past connected to highly distressing emotions.

Vanity Excessive pride about one's appearance or one's achievements, or alternatively excessive concern about these.

Common medications

Alprazolam A benzodiazepine prescribed for panic, generalised anxiety, phobias, social anxiety and OCD.

Amitriptyline A tricyclic antidepressant.

Atenolol A beta blocker prescribed for anxiety.

Buspirone A mild tranquilliser prescribed for generalised anxiety, OCD and panic.

Chlordiazepoxide A benzodiazepine prescribed for generalised anxiety and phobias.

Citalopram A selective serotonin reuptake inhibitor commonly prescribed for mixed anxiety and depression.

Clomipramine A tricyclic antidepressant.

Clonazepam A benzodiazepine prescribed for panic, generalised anxiety, phobias and social anxiety.

Desipramine A tricyclic antidepressant.

Diazepam A benzodiazepine prescribed for generalised anxiety, panic and phobias.

Doxepin A tricyclic antidepressant.

Duloxetine A serotonin-norepinephrine reuptake inhibitor.

Escitalopram Oxalate A selective serotonin reuptake inhibitor.

Fluoxetine A selective serotonin reuptake inhibitor.

Fluvoxamine A selective serotonin reuptake inhibitor.

Gabapentin An anticonvulsant prescribed for generalised anxiety and social anxiety.

Imipramine A tricyclic antidepressant.

Lorazepam A benzodiazepine prescribed for generalised anxiety, panic and phobias.

Nortriptyline A tricyclic antidepressant.

Oxazepam A benzodiazepine prescribed for generalised anxiety and phobias.

Paroxetine A selective serotonin reuptake inhibitor.

Phenelzine A monoamine oxidase inhibitor.

Pregabalin An anticonvulsant prescribed for generalised anxiety disorder.

Propanalol A beta blocker prescribed for anxiety.

Sertraline A selective serotonin reuptake inhibitor.

Tranylcypromine A monoamine oxidase inhibitor.

Valproate An anticonvulsant prescribed for panic.

Venlafaxine A serotonin-norepinephrine reuptake inhibitor.

Regulatory organisations in the UK

British Association of Cognitive and Behavioural
Psychotherapists
Imperial House
Hornby Street
Bury
Lancashire
BL9 5BN
Tel: 0161 705 4304
Fax: 0161 705 4306
Email: babcp@babcp.com

British Association for Counselling & Psychotherapy
BACP House
15 St John's Business Park
Lutterworth
LE17 4HB
Tel: 01455 883300

British Psychological Society
St Andrews House
48 Princess Road East
Leicester
LE1 7DR
Tel: +44 (0)116 254 9568
Fax: +44 (0)116 227 1314
Email: enquiries@bps.org.uk

Health & Care Professional Council
Park House
184 Kennington Park Road
London
SE11 4BU
Tel: 0300 500 6184

References and further reading

Arnsten, A., Raskind, M., Taylor, F. & Connor, D. *Neuro-biology of Stress* (2015) The effects of stress exposure on prefrontal cortex: Translating basic research into successful treatments for post-traumatic stress disorder, pp. 89–99.

Bandura, A. (1977) *Social Learning Theory*. Prentice-Hall.

Beck, J. (2011) *Cognitive Behavior Therapy: Second Edition – Basics and Beyond*. The Guildford Press.

Butler, G. (2009) *Overcoming Social Anxiety & Shyness*. Robinson.

Cabral, R. & Nardi, E. (2012) Anxiety and inhibition of panic attacks within translational and prospective research contexts. *Trends in Psychiatry*.

Clark, D.M. (1986) A cognitive approach to panic. *Behaviour Research and Therapy*, 24: 461–470.

Clark, D.M. & Wells, A. (1995) A cognitive model of social phobia. In *Social Phobia – Diagnosis, Assessment, and Treatment* (eds. R.G. Heimberg, M.R. Liebowitz, D. Hope et al.), pp. 69–93. New York: Guilford.

Debiec, J. & Sullivan, R. (2014) Intergenerational transmission of emotional trauma through amygdala-dependent mother-to-infant transfer of specific fear. *Proceedings of the National Academy of Sciences*, DOI: 10.1073/pnas.1316740111.

Golman, D. (1996). *Emotional Intelligence: Why It Can Matter More Than IQ*. Bloomsbury.

Greenberger, D. & Padesky, C. (1995) *Mind Over Mood: Change How You Feel by Changing the Way That You Think*. Guildford Press.

Guzmán, Y., Tronson, N., Jovasevic, K., Sato, K., Guedea, A., Mizukami, H., Nishimori, K. & Radulovic. J. (2013) Fear-enhancing effects of septal oxytocin receptors. *Nature Neuroscience*, 2013; DOI: 10.1038/nn.3465.

Kennerley, H. (2009) *Overcoming Anxiety: A Self-Help Guide Using Cognitive Behavioural Techniques*. Robinson.

Kinman, G. & Grant, L. (2010) Exploring stress resilience in trainee social workers: The role of emotional and social competencies. *British Journal of Social Work*, 10.1093/bjsw/bcq088.

Krusemark, E. & Li. W. (2012) Enhanced olfactory sensory perception of threat in anxiety: An event-related fMRI study. *Chemosensory Perception*, 5(1): 37 DOI: 10.1007/s12078-011-9111-7.

LeDoux, J.E., Iwata, J., Cicchetti, P., Reis, D.J. (1988) Different projections of the central amygdaloid nucleus mediate autonomic and behavioral correlates of conditioned fear. *Journal of Neuroscience*, Jul;8(7): 2517–29.

Logue, M.W., Bauver, S.R., Kremen, W.S., Franz, C.E., Eisen, S.A., Tsuang, M.T., Grant, M.D. & Lyons, M.J. (2011) Evidence of overlapping genetic diathesis of panic attacks and gastrointestinal disorders in a sample of male twin pairs. *Twin Research and Human Genetics*, Feb; 14(1): 16–24. doi: 10.1375/twin.14.1.16

Markus, H. & Nurius, P. (1986) Possible selves. *American Psychologist*, 41 (9), 954–969.

McIlrath, D. & Huitt, W. (1995) The teaching-learning process: A discussion of models. *Educational Psychology Interactive*. Valdosta, GA: Valdosta State University. Retrieved 2016 from: http://www.edpsycinteractive.org/papers/modeltch.html

Moorey, S. (2010) The six cycles maintenance model: Growing a 'vicious flower' for depression. *Behaviour and Cognitive Psychotherapy*, Mar; 38(2): 173–84.

Moulding, R., Coles, M.E., Abramowitz, J.S., Alcolado, G.M., Alonso, P., Belloch, A., Bouvard, M., Clark, D.A., Doron, G., Fernández-Álvarez, H., García-Soriano, G., Ghisi, M., Gómez, B., Inozu, M., Radomsky, A.S., Shams, G., Sica, C., Simos, G. & Wong, W. (2014) Part 2. They scare because we care: the relationship between obsessive intrusive thoughts and appraisals and control strategies across 15 cities. *Journal of Obsessive-Compulsive and Related Disorders*, 3(3): 280–291.

Rachman, S., Coughtrey, S.R. & Radomsky, A. (2015) *The Oxford Guide to the Treatment of Mental Contamination*. The Oxford University Press.

Seger, C.A. (2011) A critical review of habit learning and the basal ganglia. *Frontiers in Systems Neuroscience*, Aug 30; 5:66.

Teachman, B., Marker, C. & Clerkin, E. (2010) Catastrophic misinterpretations as a predictor of symptom change during treatment for panic disorder. *Journal of Consulting and Clinical Psychology*, 78(6): 964–973.

Veale, D., & Wilson, R. (2005) *Overcoming Obsessive Compulsive Disorder: A Self-help Guide using Cognitive Behavioral Techniques*. Constable & Robinson Ltd.

Wells, A. (1997) *Cognitive Therapy of Anxiety Disorders: A Practice Manual and Conceptual Guide*. Wiley.

Scoring for compulsions questionnaire

Cleansing compulsions

(8, 15, 17, 24, 27, 32)

8. Over-washing hands or body through bathing or showering. Needing to wash in a particular way.

15. Overuse of particular sprays or disinfectants.

17. Avoiding coming into contact with people, places or particular items that are viewed as contaminated, or throwing away things that have been contaminated.

24. Wearing gloves to avoid contamination

27. Over-cleaning household items or objects.

32. Over-cleaning particular areas of the house.

Ordering and repeating compulsions

(1, 9, 19, 25, 31, 33)

1. Arranging things in the environment or the mind in a certain order.

9. Mental rehearsal of the same cognitions over and over again, or saying the same things over and over again like a mantra.

19. Completing specific activities a specific number of times, touching safe objects, superstitious behaviour that takes up a lot of time.

25. Writing and rewriting things.

31. Counting and recounting items, for example, money or other objects.

33. Reading and re-reading things to make sure that they have been understood correctly.

Appearance compulsions

(3, 10, 18, 29, 36, 38)

3. Deliberately thinking of ways to avoid situations where perceived physical defect/s may be more noticeable.

10. Photographing perceived defect/s, looking in the mirror using many different angles to inspect perceived defect/s.

18. Checking body for particular perceived defect/s.

29. Altering appearance, adjusting appearance to hide perceived defect/s.

36. Excessive use of make-up to hide perceived defect/s.

38. Requesting repeated reassurance about appearance of perceived defect/s from others.

Unknown illness compulsions

(6, 11, 21, 28, 34, 39)

6. Mentally repetitively inspecting scenarios where perceived illness could have been contracted, for example, sexually transmitted diseases such as AIDS, hepatitis, etc.

11. Continuously checking the self or loved ones with medical devices, e.g., blood pressure machine, thermometer, etc.

21. Spending large amounts of time on the internet researching disease connected to the self or loved ones.

28. Continuously requesting reassurance about the health of the self or loved ones from others.

34. Requesting repeated medical tests for the self or loved ones.

39. Continuously checking the self or loved ones for pulse, heart rate, checking heart rate for an irregular beat.

Hoarding compulsions

(2, 5, 7, 30, 35, 40)

2. Buying things that are not really needed for fear of running out.

5. Saving or collecting items that don't really need to be saved.

7. Keeping items as they may one day become useful.

30. Keeping paperwork just in case it contains something that may be missed or important.

35. Picking up useless items from the ground.

40. Continuously refreshing memories to ensure that they are intact.

Forgiveness compulsions

(4, 14, 20, 22, 41, 42)

4. Seeking reassurance as a result of having bad thoughts about others.

14. Acts of self-harm such as picking skin or self-mutilation to counteract bad thoughts.

20. Behaviours designed to counteract bad thoughts.

22. Need to confess to somebody about thoughts.

41. Completing mental rituals to counteract bad thoughts.

42. Praying for forgiveness after having bad thoughts about others.

Checking compulsions

(12, 13, 16, 23, 26, 37)

12. Checking and rechecking the same internet pages to make sure that nothing has changed – e.g. Facebook – or continuously listening to the news to make sure that nothing has happened to loved ones.

13. Checking journeys you have taken, retracing steps, going back to somewhere you have already been to check that everything is in order.

16. Checking that physical things are in order, e.g., doors, cars, appliances, jars, plugs, wallets, purses, bags, mobile phones, lockers to make sure things are as they should be.

23. Continuously phoning or texting relatives or loved one to check that they are OK.

26. Checking doors, locks and windows to make sure they are locked.

37. Continuous checking of emails, texts or other communication devices to make sure that you have not missed anything.

Interpretation of scores

You can add up your scores on this inventory and use them as a guide. The areas where you score more highly will be where you need to focus on reducing your compulsive behaviours.

Feelings exercise

- Begin by noticing where you feel your emotion most strongly.

- Keep your focus on your feeling. Place your hand on the place where you feel your emotion more strongly. You are placing your hand on your body where your emotion is, because many of us who are prone to avoiding emotions unconsciously and automatically move away from feeling emotions go into our heads instead. You are gaining a connection with your emotions and keeping your focus on how you are feeling. Placing your hand on the part of your body where you feel your anxiety more strongly will also act as a reminder to you to keep your focus on your emotions. It is very important while you are doing this exercise to focus on feeling your feelings and remind yourself that you really are willing for your emotions to be there.

- Focusing on the part of your body underneath your hand with your mind, examine exactly what your emotion feels like. For example, how much space do your feelings take up? How painful or uncomfortable are your feelings? Rate the intensity of your feeling between 1 and 10, where 10 is the highest level of intensity. While you continue to feel your feelings, mentally give your feelings permission to take up the space that they are taking up in your body. If you want to take things a little further you could also speak to your distress. Internally, say something along the lines of 'Thank you for being there' or 'There are very good reasons for you being there.' Remember the idea that from the primitive mind's point of view there is a good reason for your anxiety being there, even if it does not make sense logically. Follow that by saying 'You are welcome to stay there for as long as you want.'

- Bear in mind that, from the sub-cortical region's (primitive mind's) point of view, if it notices during its screening process that there is a cue to a potential threat, whether physical or psychological, it is just doing its job properly if it brings the threat to your attention and helps you to prepare. The threat does not need to be logical, real or valid in the current time mode. If it has been perceived as a threat in the past, or you have previously confirmed the existence of the threat by withdrawing from this threat in the past then, from the primitive mind's point of view, the threat is still active.

- While feeling your symptoms of anxiety it is important when you speak to your feelings that you really mean what you are saying. Let go of all your thoughts and focus on your feeling. The importance of your self-communication is not in the words that you use but rather the intention behind your words. Keep an idea in mind of accepting, recognising, being grateful and being patient. Do this for a minute or so and bring your awareness to what happens.

- Stay with your emotions as the intensity gradually decreases.

- It is important in the early stages of CBT when you are experiencing anxiety, low mood, guilt and anger to practise being with these feelings as much as possible. This will help you in two ways.

158

First, it will help you to fear your feelings less; second, it will make it more likely that you will be able to use this acceptance approach when you are experiencing higher levels of distress.

- Bear in mind that in a state of heightened distress the frontal lobes, where most of our logical thinking occurs, stop working somewhat. Doing the same thing over and over again when you are not so distressed will make it more likely that you will be able to access and use this approach automatically when you really need it.